Collector's Originality Guide
MUSTANG
1964 1/2–1966

Collector's Originality Guide
MUSTANG
1964 1/2–1966

COLIN DATE

motorbooks

First published in 2002 by Motorbooks, an imprint of MBI Publishing Company, 400 First Avenue North, Suite 300, Minneapolis, MN 55401 USA

Motorbooks titles are also available at discounts in bulk quantity for industrial or sales-promotional use. For details write to Special Sales Manager at MBI Publishing Company, 400 First Avenue North, Suite 300, Minneapolis, MN 55401 USA.

To find out more about our books, visit us online at www.motorbooks.com.

Originally published in hardcover as *Original Mustang 1964 1/2–1966.*

Library of Congress Cataloging-in-Publication Data

Date, Colin, 1956-
  Collector's Originality Guide Mustang 1964-1/2-1966 / Colin Date.
      p. cm.
  Rev. ed. of: Original Mustang, 1964-1/2-1966. St. Paul : MBI, 2002.
  Includes index.
  ISBN 978-0-7603-3745-5 (sb)
  1. Mustang automobile—History. 2. Mustang automobile—Conservation and restoration. I. Date, Colin, 1956- Original Mustang, 1964-1/2-1966. II. Title.
  TL215.M8D38 2009
  629.222'2—dc22
                                                            2009023426

On the cover: Only 1.3 percent of 1965 Mustang buyers purchased the high-performance K-code engine option. The Dual Red Band nylon tires were standard with the K-code option, while the fog lamps were part of the GT Equipment group. *David Newhardt*

On the frontispiece: Markings that easily distinguish the GT Mustangs include special body-side striping and a GT emblem.

On the title page: The spectacular K-code 1965 GT fastback wears paint code A: Raven Black.

On the table of contents page: This is an early 1965 production A-code convertible in Poppy Red.

On the back cover: The incredible 1965 Shelby GT-350.

About the author
Colin Date was born and raised in Toronto, Canada. There he worked in the advertising and marketing field, primarily in the retail packaged goods industry. After relocating to Oregon in 1994, Colin became involved in the automotive publishing realm, writing and shooting numerous features for magazines, including *Chevy High Performance*, *Mustang Monthly*, *Mopar Muscle,* and *Muscle Car Review*. Today, Colin and his family reside in southern California.

Editor: Peter Bodensteiner
Designer: Chris Fayers
Cover designer: Kou Lor

Printed in China

Contents

Foreword
by Donald Farr

On January 11, 1966, a brand-new Mustang GT suddenly appeared in my grandparents' driveway, right across Highway 49 from my house. I know the exact date because, as a 13-year-old, I kept a somewhat scraggly diary of all the events in my young life, like buying a new Beatle album or taking a girlfriend to see a James Bond movie. But January 11 was a special entry because, as it turned out, my grandfather had traded in his staid four-door Falcon for the Mustang, a Signalflare Red coupe with a white vinyl roof. Nothing was groovier than being 13 and riding around town in a new Mustang!

It seems that everyone has a first-generation Mustang story to tell. For some, it was a first car, either new or used. For others, it was the cool car that belonged to a neighbor down the street. Many remember cruising in a Mustang owned by a friend of a friend.

One thing is perfectly obvious—people remember 1964½ through 1966 Mustangs because they were cool cars, and cool to be seen in. Much better than hiding in the back seat of your buddy's father's Galaxie four-door.

Of course, the Mustang is the car that started it all. The 1964½ Mustang, although little more than a sporty restyled Falcon, not only established sales records, it also created a new category of American vehicle. Where else would the term *ponycar* come from? Without the first-generation Mustang, it's doubtful that we would have seen the Camaro, Firebird, Javelin, 'Cuda, or Challenger.

For a little more than two years—from its introduction on April 17, 1964, until the last of the '66s were produced in August of 1966—the first-generation Mustangs flooded the streets and driveways of America. More than 400,000 were sold in 1965 to set a record for a first full year of production. Eventually, production figures topped 1 million by the end of the 1966 model year. The first-generation cars established the Mustang as an American icon, as noted when a 1964½ Mustang was chosen to represent the 1960s for a U.S. postage stamp in 1999. The legacy continues today, some 36 years after those first long-hood, short-deck Mustangs were introduced.

My friend Colin Date's new book, *Original Mustang 1964½–1966*, which you hold in your hands, will revive memories. It serves as a historical point of reference as well as a loose guide for restorers in their attempts to re-create the original Mustang as it came from the factory. You'll no doubt spot Mustangs in here that will rekindle a thought or two about a 1964½–1966 Mustang from your past, whether it was your first car or the car you craved in your neighbor's driveway.

Or if you were lucky like me, it was in your grandfather's driveway.

Acknowledgments

It took an incredible amount of time and information from many different sources to complete this book. My sincerest thanks for the efforts of the following people:

Shannon Murray, Mark Mosteller, Paul Segura, Steve Grant, and Brett Stierli who provided answers to my endless stream of questions, and offered their stunning Mustangs for dissection and photographic purposes.

Tom Shaw, editor of *Musclecar Power* magazine, for his photographic contributions. The Tropical Turquoise 1965 fastback and stunning 1966 Shelby GT-350 convertible in this book are both examples of Tom's handiwork.

Donald Farr, past editor of numerous Mustang and Ford publications, and current editor of mustangweekly.com, for contributing his foreword to this book.

David Osborn, of Jim Osborn Reproductions, Inc., for supplying the plethora of historic information contained in their publications on 1964½ through 1966 Mustangs.

Bob Mannel, author of *Mustang & Ford Small Block V-8: 1962–1969*, for his invaluable guide to charting the eight-cylinder engine changes throughout the sixties.

Jim Smart and Jim Haskell, for the incredible amount of production facts and figures in their best-selling handbook *Mustang Production Guide Volume 1, 1964–1966*.

Tony Gregory, author of *The 289 High Performance Mustang*, for all the minute details that distinguish the mighty K-coded cars from their V-8 brethren.

The authors and publishers of the *1965–1968 Mustang & Shelby Parts Identifier*, for a wonderful compilation of part and tag numbers—mandatory reading for "getting it right."

My editor, Peter Bodensteiner, who came on midstream in this project, got up to speed, and helped me through my fast-approaching deadline.

Motorbooks International, for giving me the opportunity of a lifetime writin' and shootin' my own book.

My wonderful wife Dianne, son Steve, and daughter Kim for their undying support and patience as I spent many a night shut up in my room full of textbooks and shop manuals.

Scott Hamm for his help with six- and eight-cylinder engine research.

All the enthusiastic people who volunteered not only their beautiful cars, but their time as well: Dennis and Karen Hart, Scott King, Bob Fria, Whit and Julie Anderson, Stephen Nemeth, Dick East, Larry King, Richard Kaneshiro, Tony Sousa, and Darren Smith.

A special thank-you to the good Lord, who has guided me every step of the way.

Introduction

We all remember where we were when we saw our first Mustang. In the spring of 1964 I was an impressionable young lad of 7, living in suburban Toronto. I had been a car freak since I was 3 years old, and the day I saw a billboard advertising Ford's latest creation, that was it for me. The 40-foot-wide poster featured a dazzling illustration of the new car: a sleek blue convertible blasting down the freeway, seemingly in its own space and time. It was the day my fascination with sweeping land yachts and tail fins waned and I became a sports car junkie. Within a few weeks, I was building a 1/25th scale model of my own Mustang. My spare time was spent clipping the local Ford dealer's ads and pasting pictures on my bedroom walls. While my car buddies and I were frantically trying to figure out how to get our driver's licenses early, we were also scheming ways to bankroll one of these beauties (the lawns in our neighborhood never looked neater). I couldn't convince my dad to buy one ("too expensive and not practical"), so I had to admire Ford's hot new machines from afar. When the new Mustangs started rolling on Toronto streets, I remember heads turning and people whistling. I didn't realize it at the time, but I was witnessing the birth of the ponycar legend.

It all started with Ford's massive kickoff on April 17, 1964. The new Mustangs smashed all sales records by selling an unheard of 22,000 units the very first day, and another 241,434 by year's end. By the time April 17, 1965, had rolled around, 418,812 ponycars were sitting in various North American driveways. The sales numbers this car generated are astounding, and its historical significance was even more so.

The first-generation Mustangs totally dominated the sport compact segment of the automobile industry and ruled the road with very little competition. Ford's timing couldn't have been better. Chrysler was making a mild splash with its new Valiant variant, the Barracuda (23,443 cars hit the streets in 1964), and GM was way off in the sidelines with its mostly unsuccessful and trouble-plagued Corvair. It wouldn't be until 1967 that GM and Chrysler would even begin to play catch-up with the wildly successful Mustang. From its 1964½ introduction through the 1966 model year, first-generation 'Stangs literally set the benchmark for others to follow. The coupes, convertibles, fastbacks, GTs, K-codes, and Shelby cars set the world on fire. With the Mustang, Ford changed the face of the buying public forever.

Although I have been a car fanatic for at least 40 years, only since 1999 have I been privileged to author and photograph in the automotive industry. My career in graphic design and marketing since 1975 primarily focused on the design and promotion of packaged goods. Back in 1999, the editor of *Muscle Car Review* magazine, Tom Shaw, gave me the opportunity to take a crack at "shootin' and writin'." I took a 1970 GTO Judge out to the Columbia River Gorge in northern Oregon and did a travelog-type feature for the magazine. That was it. I was hooked. Two years (and about 45 various magazine features) later, I find myself writing a book on my early-childhood love, 1964½ through 1966 Mustangs. Over the past couple of years I photographed (and road-tested) everything from big-block 'Cudas and Cougars to COPO Camaros. Not until I sat down to write this book did it fully dawn on me that the Mustang was really the car that started it all.

In my relatively short career as a freelance automotive journalist, I have found that one of the biggest stumbling blocks is finding cars that are stock in appearance and content. This challenge applies to all vintage muscle cars. To find a car (whatever the marque) in stock original condition (whether it's a genuine survivor or a meticulously restored example) is a rare occurrence. The number of classic cars out there that have been modified over the years is staggering. Although modification can be a positive thing, it tends to water down the breed, and the authenticity of the vehicle and its historic significance get lost in the translation. First-generation Mustangs are no exception. I guess sometimes it is just about impossible to leave well enough alone, which brings me to the entire point of this book.

Mustangs were not perfect cars right off the assembly line. Never have been, never will be. They do, however, represent an exciting, romantic lifestyle and automotive passion that few other cars were ever able to emulate. As stated earlier, and as most of you probably already know, the sales and production numbers that Ford generated with the new Mustangs were overwhelming. What you may not be aware of, however, is that fewer than 5 percent of these cars remain in stock, original (read: unmodified) condition today.

Original Mustang 1964½–1966 is all about keeping the legend alive. It offers a historical point of reference and describes the early Mustangs, before "modification" became a household word. These pages feature either immaculately restored show cars or unmolested originals, with the sole emphasis on detailed authenticity for the purposes of restoration.

This book is dedicated to the men and women committed to preserving the Mustang bloodline.

1966 Mustang convertible in Candyapple Red.

Chapter 1

Mustang Primer:
Understanding the Basics

Back in the early 1960s, Lee Iacocca was acting as vice president and general manager of Ford. Iacocca, an engineer, sales/marketing guru, and all-around car guy, had worked his way up through the ranks at Ford fairly quickly. With the advent of Chevrolet's Monza and 300-horsepower Chryslers hitting the streets, Iacocca knew something had to be done, and fast. Ford's only specialty car was the relatively expensive Thunderbird, and its target audience was something else altogether. Working with chief engineers Bob Negstad, Hal Sperlich, and a host of other dedicated professionals, Iacocca scrambled together a think-tank dream team. Concept after concept emerged, including the legendary mid-engined Mustang I introduced in October 1962. In 1963, the hot Mustang II show car made headlines. Finally, after analyzing all the options and taking into account the fiscal ramifications, the decision was made to tweak the lowly but highly

Left, right, and below: Comparison views of the three model years. The 1964½ (right) and 1965 (opposite) model Mustangs featured a honeycomb-style grille finished in gunmetal gray, while 1966 cars (below) moved to an extruded aluminum grille with bright horizontal bars. Officially introduced in April 1965, the GT models were distinguished (among other things) by a pair of fog lights located inside the grille. Hood lip moldings were first introduced on the 1965 GTs, then became standard equipment on all 1966 Mustangs.

successful Falcon. The engineers slipped the Falcon a few Fairlane parts here and there (including the Fairlane's new 221-ci V-8), slowly morphing it into the Falcon "Sprint." The resulting "compact car with a V-8 engine" proved too enticing to resist. Ford then designed a sexy new body and adapted it to a lightly modified Falcon platform. Because the Falcon's tooling was already available, it would be relatively easy and incredibly economical to use most of that car's underpinnings. When executives realized that the new car could be sold for less than $2,500, they gave it the green light. Essentially, first-generation Mustangs were Falcons with modified Mustang II bodies.

Ford's marketing strategy was a simple one: offer the public a nicely equipped car with plenty of style, comfort, and convenience features. Then, let them customize it to their heart's content. For power and performance, you could order your car with either six or eight cylinders, ranging from 101 horsepower all the way up to 271. Most of Ford's competition offered six cylinders only, or V-8 power only. For style and convenience, first-generation Mustangs came equipped with many standard features that were optional on other cars.

Production

The 1964½–1966 Mustangs were manufactured by Ford Motor Company, USA, at assembly plants located in Dearborn, Michigan; Metuchen, New Jersey; and San Jose, California. Mustangs from each of the production facilities were designated a DSO (District Sales Office) code to indicate in which area of the country they would be sold.

Production began on March 9, 1964, at the Dearborn plant and ended August 12, 1966, at the same facility. Over the three model years, 1,288,557 Mustangs were built and shipped to various locations worldwide.

The first Mustangs were available as coupes, fastbacks, and convertibles. They were all constructed in the same fashion: the body is an all-welded unit attached to a platform-type chassis. Although the models offer obvious design differences, hardtops and convertibles were essentially the same. According to Ford Motor Company archives, the first mass production unit was a Wimbledon White convertible with a black vinyl interior, sporting the maiden vehicle identification number 5F08F100001.

From March 9 until June 19, 1964, the Dearborn plant manufactured both Mustangs and Fairlanes. During the first official week of Mustang production, they completed 867 units. At the end of the following week, with production stepped up considerably, 1,955 cars were completed. As the weeks passed, the general public fell into an

The 1964½ and 1965 models (left) share the same simulated air scoop on the rear quarter panels. The GT models (1965, opposite, and 1966) dispensed with the chrome scoop edging, leaving a smooth, sculptured look. In 1966 (above), the standard scoop added a little more flash, "enhancing the Mustang's look of fleetness and motion," according to sales literature.

all-out Mustang feeding frenzy. Dearborn started cranking out 75 ponycars each hour, or approximately 1,200 units per day. By July of 1964, public demand literally overwhelmed supply. Dealers were taking orders for cars that regularly took more than four months to fill. Although production topped out at more than 7,000 cars per month, it still wasn't enough to keep up!

By July 13, 1964, Ford's San Jose plant sent their Fairlane and Falcon manufacturing business elsewhere and took on Mustang production full-time. By the end of the 1964 calendar year, demand for the new cars was so staggering that Ford elected to start production at their plant in Metuchen, New Jersey. On February 1, 1965, less than a year after initial Mustang production began, the third assembly plant joined in the attempt to meet demand for the Mustang.

Model Years

Some sources claim that no 1964½ cars exist, only early 1965s. This statement contains a bit of truth. You won't find a Mustang bearing a 1964 model year VIN (vehicle identification number) or one officially titled as a 1964 (all early Mustangs bore a "1965" VIN). Still, they were manufactured at the same time as other 1964 Fords, which actually makes them 1964-era production vehicles.

Other than the midyear introduction of the first Mustangs, the cars were typically built five months prior to the calendar year. Truth be told, many distinct differences separate the three model years, which we will illustrate throughout this book.

Body/Chassis Construction

Instead of the typical body-on-frame-rails construction, Ford touted its "new" concept platform chassis to its sales force and the buying public alike. (In actuality, the chassis was just a modification of the existing Falcon unit.) "Strong and highly resistant to twisting," read the literature. The "platform" consisted of boxed front and rear side rails tied to heavily boxed rocker panels. Five heavy-gauge cross-members connected the basic platform sections, forming a ladder-type frame. The floor pan was then welded to the front and rear side rails. The full-length transmission/driveshaft tunnel incorporated in the floor pan gave the entire structure stiffness and rigidity. The engine compartment also added strength to the new car, with full-depth side panels (inner fender wells) welded to the front side rails and to the cowl area.

Body construction of the new Mustang was engineered to deliver maximum strength without adding unnecessary weight. The car's sleek new shape came from an all-welded unit that was in

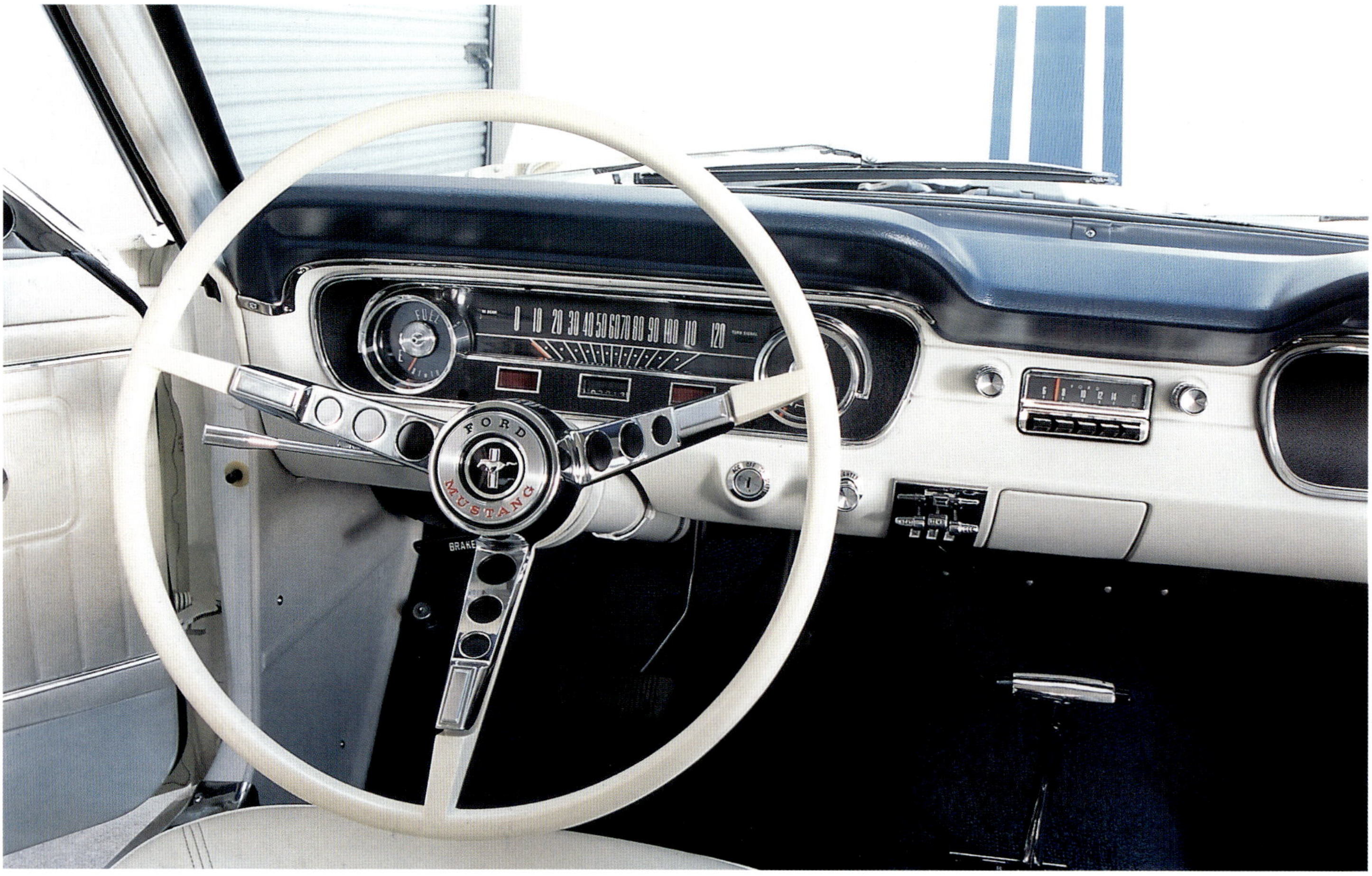
FORD
MUSTANG
BRAKE

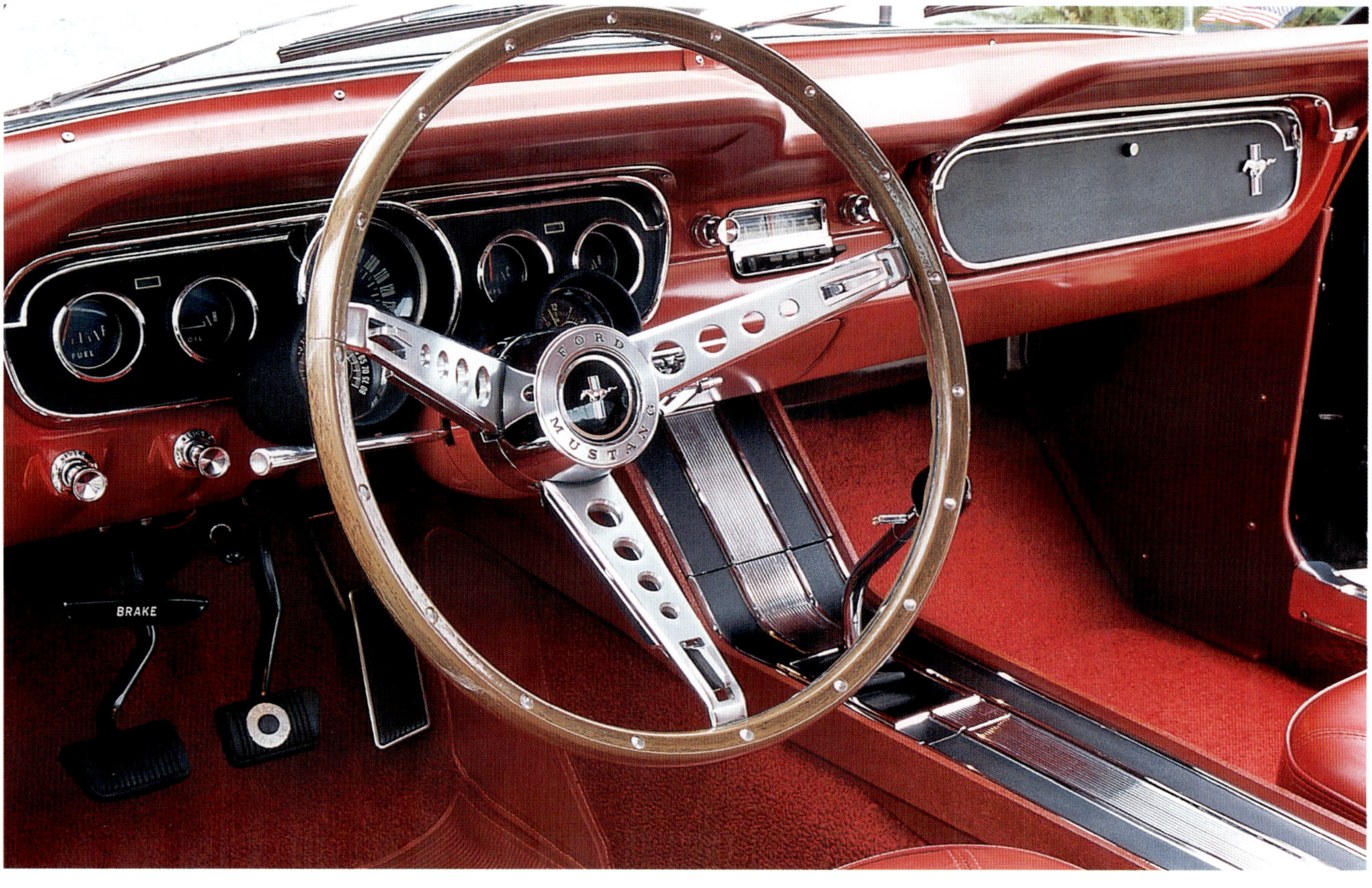
FORD
MUSTANG
BRAKE
FUEL
OIL

A major difference among the model years was the instrument panel: 1964½ (opposite above) and 1965 standard equipment instrument clusters featured a rectangular speedometer layout, flanked by fuel and temperature gauges. In 1965, Mustangs equipped with either the GT package (opposite below) or interior decor group sported a centrally located round speedometer with fuel and oil gauges to the left, and ammeter and temperature gauges on the right. In 1966 (above), all Mustangs went to the five-gauge layout.

turn welded to the platform chassis. As the original literature stated: "All framing around the body openings and the roof bracing are either of box, channel, or hat section design." For added strength, all structural surfaces and panels were made from large stampings to reduce the number of smaller welds. Because the body was originally designed to be a convertible, the necessary rigidity was planned from the start. Adding a hardtop to the car simply increased its overall strength.

Corrosion Protection

Ford also touted the corrosion protection of its new cars. Early promotional literature explained: "Extensive steps have been taken in the design and manufacture of the Mustang to provide a longer lasting body with maximum protection against corrosion from road salts and moisture. All interior body areas are vented to help prevent entrapment of moisture. In addition, zinc-rich primer is applied to lower interior portions of the various body panels, doors, pillars, and to the splash areas of the wheel housings. Certain members of the body and platform chassis utilize Zinclad steel where maximum corrosion protection is required. Zinclad steel is standard steel with a heavy coating of zinc applied. In all, 26 pieces of the platform and body are manufactured of

PRODUCTION 1964½, 1965 & 1966

1964½ CARS
March 9, 1964: Production begins at Dearborn, Michigan
July 13, 1964: Production begins at San Jose, California
July 31, 1964: Last documented build date for 1964½ cars at Dearborn and San Jose
Production totaled 121,538 units
Model breakdown: Coupes: 92,705; Convertibles: 28,833

1965 CARS
August 1, 1964: Production begins at Dearborn and San Jose
February 1, 1965: Production begins at Metuchen, New Jersey
July 31, 1965: Last documented build date for 1965 cars at Dearborn
August 13, 1965: Last documented build date for 1965 cars at Metuchen
August 20, 1965: Last documented build date for 1965 cars at San Jose
Production totaled 559,451 units
Model breakdown: Coupes: 409,260; Fastbacks: 77,079; Convertibles: 73,112

1966 CARS
August 16, 1965: Production begins at Dearborn and San Jose
August 25, 1965: Production begins at Metuchen
July 27, 1966: Last documented build date for 1966 cars at Metuchen
July 29, 1966: Last documented build date for 1966 cars at San Jose
August 12, 1966: Last documented build date for 1966 cars at Dearborn
Production totaled 607,568 units
Model breakdown: Coupes: 499,751; Fastbacks: 35,698; Convertibles: 72,119

Left: The 170-ci inline six-cylinder was the standard engine in 1964½. It is easily identified by its black engine block, red air cleaner, and red valve cover.

Below: Optional for 1964½, the 260-ci V-8 engine featured a black engine block with a blue air cleaner and blue valve covers. The 289-powered cars came with black engine blocks and gold valve covers and air cleaners, with the exception of the K-code cars. They received chrome valve covers and a chrome air cleaner.

In 1965 the new 200-ci six-cylinder sported exactly the same color scheme as its 170-ci predecessor, while V-8 engines (right) came with black blocks, gold air cleaners, and gold valve covers. K-code engines received chrome air cleaners and valve covers.

Below: 1966 engines received the "color monotone" treatment. Both six-cylinder and eight-cylinder blocks, air cleaners, and valve covers were painted the darker Ford Corporate Blue. Once again, the K-code cars featured chrome air cleaners and valve covers.

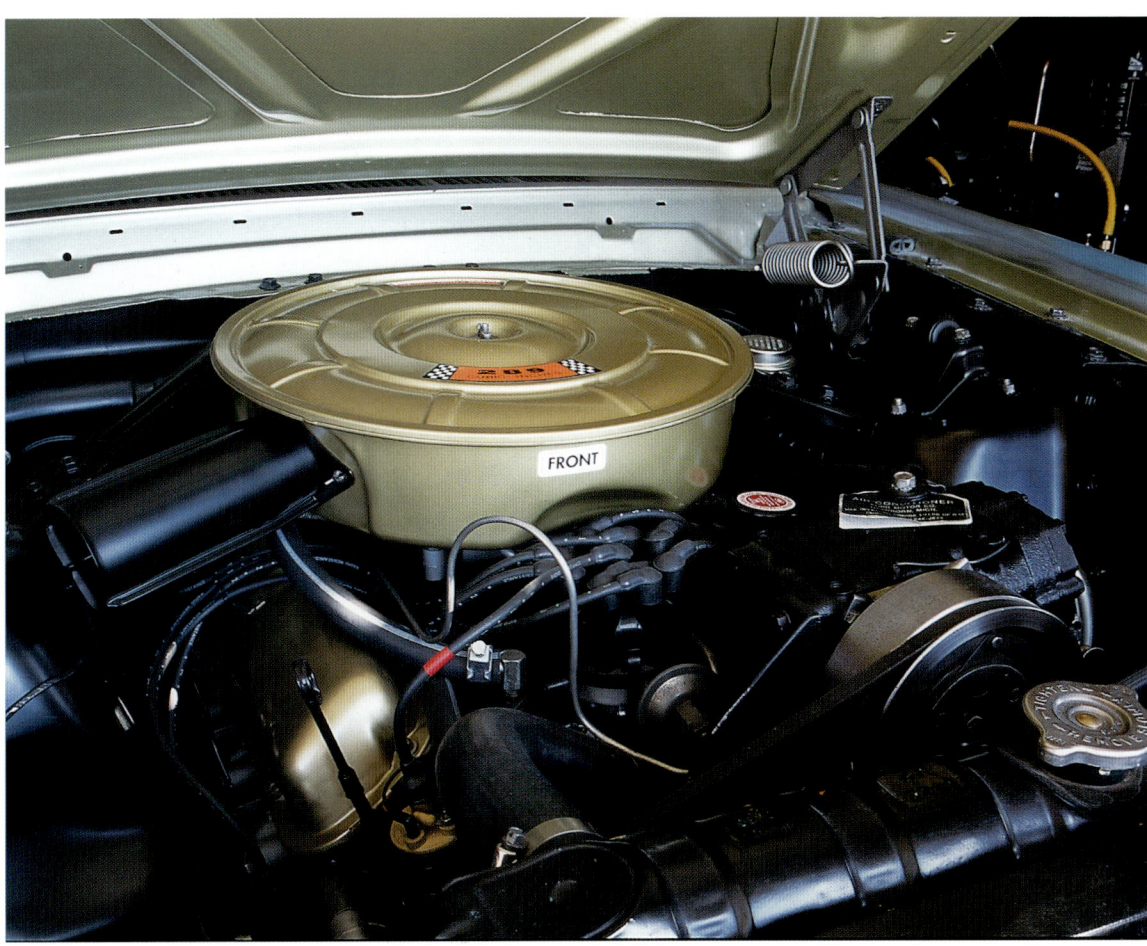

Zinclad steel. Included are the front and rear side rails, rocker panels, and the body panels beneath the front and rear bumpers. Further corrosion protection is provided by the asphalt-based sound deadener sprayed on the various body and platform panels such as doors, quarter panels, and wheel housings."

Body Insulation

Ford offered its new Mustang customers the smoothest, quietest, and most comfortable ride possible. Sales literature in 1964 boasted the following: "To help drivers and passengers enjoy their new cars to the fullest and to help reduce driver fatigue, the passenger compartment of all Mustangs is surrounded by a variety of insulating and soundproofing material, shielding occupants from road and engine noise and providing protection against weather extremes."

- Hood: Inner- and outer-panel construction, with mastic adhesive spotted between panels.
- Front fenders: Inner housing, including fender apron sprayed with sound deadener coating.
- Dash panel: One-inch amberlite pad between passengers and engine, with heavy asphalt-impregnated facing board covering.
- Cowl sides: One-quarter-inch fiberglass pads at cowl sides
- Front floor area: Extra-heavy uncured rubber mat sound deadener plus thick jute pad bonded to floor mat from toeboard to back of front seat.
- Rear floor area: Waffle-textured, asphalt-impregnated mat plus jute pad bonded to floor mat.
- Door and quarter panels: Sound deadener applied to inner surface of door outer panels.
- Rear seat area: Waffle-textured, asphalt-impregnated felt mat.
- Package tray (at rear): One-quarter-inch amberlite padding under full width of package tray covering.
- Roof panel: One-half-inch-thick fiberglass blanket insulates entire roof panel front to rear.
- Deck lid: Inner and outer panel construction, with mastic adhesive spotted between panels.
- Rear wheel housing: Splash areas sprayed with sound deadener, and cellulose pads between wheel housing and quarter panels for extra quietness.

V-8 engine designations were called out on the outermost front fenders for all three years. Six-cylinder cars received no outer badging.
Bottom right: 1964½ gas caps could easily be removed (or stolen!).

Above left and right: 1965 and 1966 caps were tethered with a braided steel cable.

Below: GT gas caps finally received a special designation for 1966 models.

Extensive use of body sealing materials included the following:

Joint sealers: Special plastic sealing material protected exposed spot-welded seams and joints. Vinyl plastic sealing compound was used at roof drip rails and the rear deck trough. Heat-curing sealer material was applied full-length to all other panel seams and joints.

Special antisqueak and sealing devices: special pads, grommets, seals, and plug buttons guarded against friction, water, dust, and drafts. The windshield and rear window were sealed with special nondrying plastic compound that retained its elasticity and kept a tight seal. Plastic shields covered inside surfaces between the metal and trim to prevent water damage to trim panels.

Assembly

In the mid-1960s, Mustangs were considered among the safest and best-built automobiles in the world. Mustang assembly was both sophisticated and simple. Because of the record rates at which the new cars were being built, Ford paid special attention to quality control. New paint areas set up in the Dearborn plant accommodated the massive increases in production, and new conveyor lines and state-of-the-art automatic welders handled platform assembly.

The new car's "engine box" or engine bay area was actually put together in a huge jig that was part of what Ford dubbed the "Merry Go-Round." Several front-end assemblies and components were built and welded together there by both human and robot welders. The rest of the Mustang was assembled at the metal shop, where the front-end assemblies, platforms, cowl vent boxes, body panels, and structural units were fabricated, mated, welded, and finished before they moved on to the paint shop. After surface prepping and painting was done, completed bodies rolled along the trim line where all electrical components, interiors, glass, and other details were applied or installed. After the trim line, the cars were fitted with their front suspensions and powertrains. Last stop was the final assembly line where completed Mustangs were lowered onto their rear axles and suspension.

Other outer markings to easily distinguish the GT Mustangs included special body side striping and a GT emblem.

Codes

By far, the most important numerical identification on first-generation Mustangs is the fender stamping containing the VIN. All 1964½–1966 Mustangs also came with a warranty plate (sometimes referred to as a patent plate or data plate) that was located on the left (driver's side) door near the latch. This plate however, simply provided a means to identify the car at a glance and to decipher the DSO, paint, trim, and other options. Because it could be removed with relatively little trouble (hence altering the car's identity), Mustang afficionados have long relied on the fender stamping as the true source of a car's authenticity. The "official" VIN stamping is located on a flange at the top of the fenderwell inside the engine compartment, on the left side of the vehicle. The VIN was also stamped on the right inner fender, hidden underneath the right outer fender. This demarcation was referred to as the confidential VIN by law enforcement agencies.

Chrome-plated "trumpeted" exhaust tips extend through the rear valance panel. Conventional rear bumper guards were omitted on GT models.

The fender stamping: this particular vehicle's code is deciphered as:

5 = 1965, the model year

R = San Jose, the assembly plant

09 = fastback body style

K = engine designation for 289-ci "hi-po"

213497 = the vehicle's consecutive unit number assigned at the production line.

After passing paint and finish quality control inspection, all Mustangs received a PAINT OK stamp of approval. Different plants applied the stamp to various locations, but they weren't always consistent. This 1965 model was given the OK in the upper cowl area.

As the assembly was being completed, line workers applied various markings in grease, chalk, or paint. Here, the red markings on the springs indicate that this particular car is a GT and is fitted with the appropriate suspension. Different levels of equipment (V-8 or six-cylinder) dictated various color-coding. Chalk pencil numbers on the frame rails are also codes identifying certain options. The X markings near the bolt heads complete a safety inspection: this marking was only applied after all nuts and bolts were checked and tightened.

HERE'S HOW TO DECIPHER THE VEHICLE IDENTIFICATION NUMBER ON FIRST-GENERATION MUSTANGS:

- The first digit of the VIN designates the model year of the car:
  5 = 1965   6 = 1966
  1964 models were also identified (and registered) with the number 5.
- The second digit designates the assembly plant:
  F = Dearborn, Michigan
  R = San Jose, California
  T = Metuchen, New Jersey
- The third and fourth digits designate the body style:
  07 = hardtop coupe
  08 = convertible
  09 = fastback
- The fifth digit designates the engine size:
  U = 170-1V six-cylinder low compression/ regular fuel/hydraulic lifters (1964 only)
  F = 260-2V V-8 low compression/regular fuel/hydraulic lifters (1964 only)
  D = 289-4V V-8 low compression/regular fuel/hydraulic lifters (1964 only)
  K = 289-4V V-8 high compression/premium fuel/mechanical lifters (all years)
  A = 289-4V V-8 high compression/ premium fuel/hydraulic lifters (1965 and 1966)
  C = 289-2V V-8 low compression/regular fuel/hydraulic lifters (1965 and 1966)
  T = 200-1V six-cylinder low compression/regular fuel/hydraulic lifters (1965 and 1966)

As with most California-built Mustangs, this San Jose car left the assembly line without an application of undercoating. Dearborn and Metuchen cars were routinely undercoated because of harsh winter climates and road salt. Note the application of different colored rings around the lower portion of the driveshaft. Further identification coding notified line workers that this part corresponded with a certain driveline application, in this instance, a K-code GT.

The warranty plate (right), located near the latch, is affixed with rivets popped directly into the door edge. The VIN is located directly beneath the trim codes and DSO. The 1966 warranty plate (below right) was downsized for 1966 Mustangs. It still contained all the vital statistics.

The series of numbers after the engine designation reflect each individual car's consecutive unit number. Consecutive unit numbers were assigned upon vehicle order and plugged into the production schedule at that time.

Elsewhere on the warranty plate, the distinct body and trim codes, paint colors, date of manufacture, axle and transmission codes, and DSOs are noted. These aspects for each individual year will be covered in their respective chapters.

Matching Numbers

For the most part, the often-heard phrase "matching numbers" means quite simply that the car's major components (engine, transmission, frame, ID tags, etc.) all contain identical VINs or serial numbers that correspond with the rest of the car. Unfortunately, first-generation Mustangs rarely provide such matches. In the term's broadest sense, the VIN that appears on the fender stamping and warranty plate should also appear on the engine block. These matching numbers are only true of the "K" code Mustangs (289 high-performance engine). In fact, the Ks were the only Mustangs that also had their VINs stamped into the transmission housing, near the driveshaft. For the rest of the Mustang family, numbers matching is not really an applicable term.

In the mid-sixties, when these cars were rolling off the assembly lines (at record-setting rates), parts were also being manufactured in panic mode. It was not uncommon to overproduce certain parts, leading to stockpiling (which could explain why I recently saw an all-original 1966 car with "1965" cast into one of its cylinder heads). This practice also led to various parts being produced with the successive model years' dates on it (as a model year crossover neared), resulting in, say, a 1965 car with 1966 coding stamped into its hood hinges.

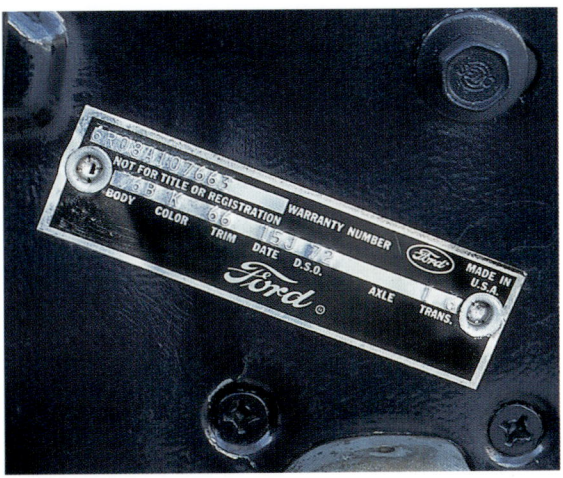

Below: (*Matching numbers*) This photo shows the VIN stamped into the engine block of a 1965 K-code Mustang. The stamping was applied at the lower portion of the block, near the oil pan. Only the hi-po K-code cars received this honor due to their rarity and propensity to theft.

Take heart restoration fans—all is not as bleak as it seems. Generally speaking, the dates affixed to most parts on first-generation cars should correspond to within two to three months of the car's build date (identified on the warranty plate). Even though Mustangs (other than the vaunted Ks) did not have an engine with a matching VIN, the engines were date-coded at the casting foundry. The Ford Motor Company utilized the alphanumeric system of "year coding" that started in the 1940s. By the time the 1960s rolled around, parts were identified as Cs (meaning the decade of the 1960s). Therefore, "C5" translates to 1965 and "C6" becomes 1966. You will find either a C5 or C6 designation cast into every Mustang engine block and transmission followed by other numbers further identifying the part. Very early cars may carry a C4 designation on certain pieces.

Beginning in January 1964, Ford equipped its engines with an engine identification tag. In this instance (1965 Mustang), it was attached by a bolt to the right side of the intake manifold. The tag stated the engine's displacement, model year, level change, year and month of manufacture, and an engine application code. At the start of the 1966 model year, an assembly plant code was introduced.

In this photo (below right), you can see the white decal applied to the engine block. The engine application code 554J matches the code on the engine identification tag. The number 554 is the code for the 1965 289 "hi-po" engine, or K-code. J is the engine suffix number assigned by Ford.

CASTING NUMBER BREAKDOWN

The following casting number breakdown shows how Ford identified many of its parts.

Decade of manufacture:
A = 1940
B = 1950
C = 1960
D = 1970

Year of decade:
The year of the decade is determined by adding a number (0–9) to the letter of the decade. Example: C6 = 1966

Car line:
A = Galaxie
D = Falcon
F = Outside USA
G = Comet/Montego
J = Industrial
M = Mercury
O = Fairlane/Torino
P = Autolite/Motorcraft
R = Rotunda
S = Thunderbird
T = Truck
V = Lincoln
Z = Mustang

Engineering departments:
A = chassis
B = body
E = engine
F = engine accessories
P = automatic transmission
R = manual transmission
W = axle
X = Muscle Parts Program
Y = Lincoln Mercury Service Parts
Z = Ford Service Parts

Every Mustang has a rear axle build tag applied at the factory to identify the axle's application, final drive ratio, date of manufacture, and plant code. In this particular case, the code stamping reads WCZ-F 3.00 4DC 901, which translates as follows: WCZ-F = 8" diameter; 3.00 = the final drive ratio of 3.00:1; 4 = 1964; D = April; C = third week (indicating an early build date); 901 = the plant code for Dearborn, Michigan cars.

Sometimes Ford's part ID numbers show up where you least expect them. And sometimes you have to be a bit of a detective to decipher them. This stamping is located on a tab underneath the front bumper: 4 7 = April 7th. M5 was an internal Ford production code.

Information was cast into every part. This photo shows the top of the radiator with the appropriate castings: C4 = 1964, the year the part was first introduced; ZE would indicate that the radiator was destined for the Mustang line; Z was commonly used to represent Mustang parts in Ford's coding system; M2 indicates that the car is equipped with an automatic transmission (Y2 would indicate a manual transmission); W-MO, or manufacturer code tells that this particular part was built in Whittier, California, by the Modine Manufacturing Company; 3 65 = March 1965, the date on which the part was actually cast.

In addition to casting numbers, all Mustangs carried certain ID tags and decals that corresponded with one another. A more prominent instance is the engine ID tag and block decal.

Build tags provided another means of identifying a component or assembly on the first-generation cars. In the photo shown on page 24, the rear axle build tag was affixed to the differential housing using one of the bolts. We cover the complete listing of rear axle build tags for the different years later in this book.

Actually, Ford's parts numbering system was pretty sophisticated for its day. Virtually every part that is bolted or welded to the car contains a number that identifies the year and item number. Most parts even identify the month and day of production. As various parts and accessories were manufactured by outside suppliers, they were logged and coded with various information that plugged directly into Ford's own network. Each of the three different manufacturing facilities located at diverse regions throughout the United States relied heavily on its own local industries for the outsourcing of various parts.

Many individual parts on first-generation Mustangs are marked with the FoMoCo and Autolite trademarks. The FoMoCo name and logo, representative of The Ford Motor Company, was used by every licensed supplier to Ford. The Autolite trademark appeared on many engine accessories (carburetors, generators, alternators, starter motors, etc.) and electronic parts and components used on early Mustangs. Autolite and its logo identity were subsidiaries of The Ford Motor Company. Rotunda, another often-heard name associated with early Mustangs, was an OE supplier that dealt primarily in accessories.

All Mustang intake manifolds had their respective IDs cast in iron. Here's how this one shakes out:

C5 = 1965;

O = Fairlane;

E = engine department;

9425 = intake manifold part number;

C = design change.

The distributor has been removed for clarification. Another example of part identification: C5 = 1965; O = Fairlane (indicates model parts interchangeability); F = engine accessories; 12127 = part number; B = application. FoMoCo also had a fairly elaborate method of dating certain parts. This distributor housing reads 5BA:
5 = 1965;
B = February, the second month of the year;
A = the first week.

Below: The steering box even has its own ID tag. The letters "HCC" would indicate the model of the steering box itself, while the "AX" indicates the application: GT only, in this instance.
AX = manual steering with a ratio of 19:1;
AW = power steering with a ratio of 16:1;
5D06B = service identification code number.

Although we cover many code "breakdowns" and further tag deciphering in subsequent chapters, we simply don't have enough room in this publication to list every Ford part and application number. Many excellent shop manuals and production guides available today identify virtually every part and accessory associated with the early Mustangs. An excellent guide to the complete engine and engine parts numbering system is *Mustang & Ford Small Block V-8 1962–1969* by Bob Mannel, published by RPM Press. Another great source for more in-depth parts identification is *1965–1968 Mustang & Shelby Parts Identifier*, published by Warner Robert Products.

Although we attempt to produce a comprehensive and accurate listing of many parts and options, this book by no means should be used as a sole source of part or casting identification.

Chapter 2

The Details:
Sweating the Small Stuff

Were the differences really all that small?

How many times have you heard someone say, "All those early Mustangs were the same." It's true that they are similar in many ways. From the basic body shape to the front end and tail lamps, you can see how the casual onlooker would have a hard time distinguishing one year from the next.

In fact most folks, even the majority of Mustang fans, will tell you there was no such thing as a 1964½ Mustang. Or if there was, it was identical to the 1965.

We devote this entire chapter to side-by-side comparison photos that distinguish the three initial years of Mustang production.

1966 Mustang GT hardtop in Ember Glo (paint code V).

Exterior

Aside from the major differences illustrated in chapter 1, several smaller changes were initiated once the 1965 model year production got underway. Some changes were designed to enhance safety and appearance. Others were merely a means to help increase production.

All exterior body panels were interchangeable between the three model years. One point of note was the absence of any fastback Mustang production during the 1964½ model year.

The traditional red, white, and blue fender emblem was there from the very beginning. Initially, the MUSTANG lettering was 4⅛ inches long, but was enlarged to 4¼ inches once the 1965 models got underway.

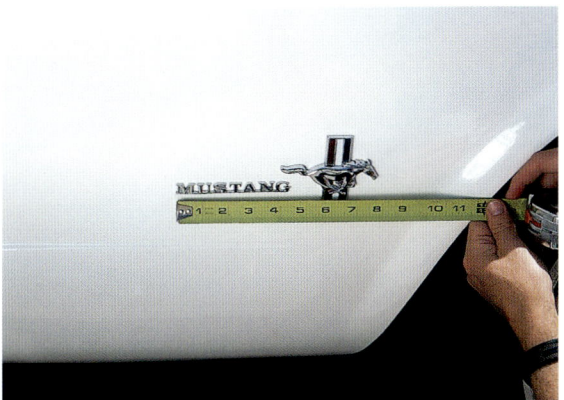

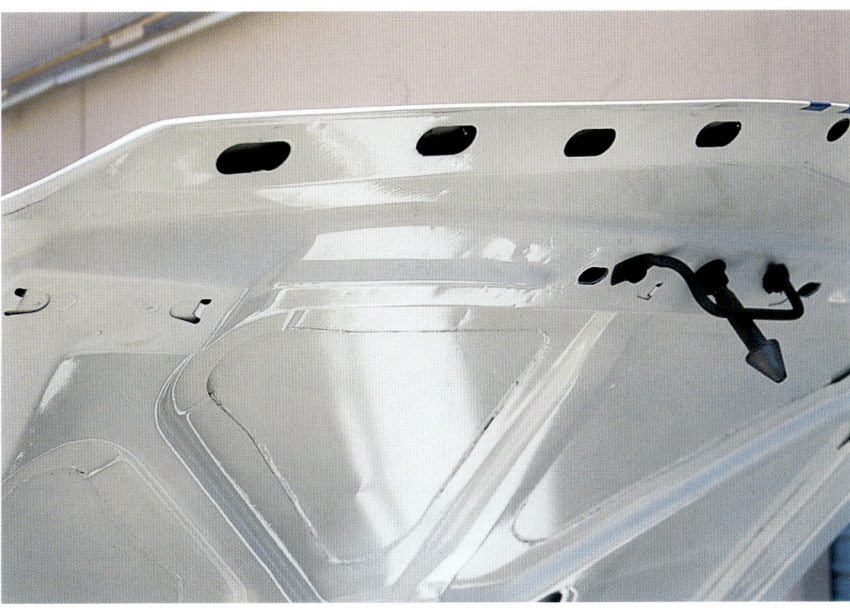

Check under the hood. The white car (above) is an early 1964½, and the red (above right) is a 1966. Other than the hood lip molding, can you spot the differences?

There are two, actually. The major difference is the reinforcement indents on the 1966 (check the upper left corner of the photo above right). Also, the 1966 hood edge flanges (at the corners) are completely sealed, and the early cars' were left open. The changes were implemented at the start of the 1965 model year.

Another grille comparison shot? No, check the beveled edge on the white car's sheet metal (left) just before the grille opening. Starting in 1965 and on through 1966, that area was "squared off" (right) for production purposes.

With the 1964½ cars, the chrome windshield wiper bezel, to which the wiper arm attaches, was mounted directly to the hood (far left). The 1965s sat out slightly (left), and that small area of the hood was molded differently to accommodate the design change.

The 1964½ and 1965 (right) Mustangs sported chrome wiper arms. They looked terrific, but glare posed a problem. Starting with the 1966 models (far right), wiper arms were made from stainless steel.

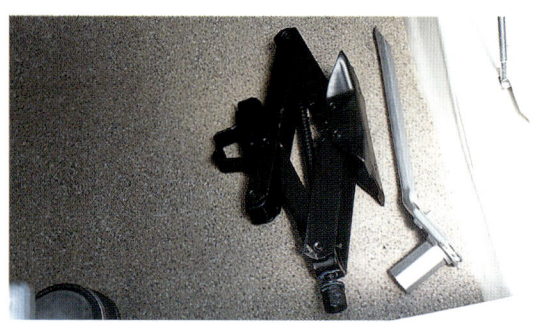 

On 1964½ (far left) models, the trunk area was covered by a fabric-backed rubber mat with a distinctive speckled texture. The 1965 and 1966 (left) cars featured full cargo area plastic mats with a distinctive cross-hatched design.

Interior

Although mostly subtle in difference, the 1965 and 1966 Mustangs varied quite significantly from their 1964½ counterparts. In the early production days of 1964, designers and engineers worked from the Falcon parts bin, and jerry-rigged many parts and procedures to accommodate the new Mustang's design. As the year progressed and the 1965 models started production, many interior details were modified and finessed, mostly for the sake of aesthetics. As more and more options were introduced, things like door panels and dash bezels changed to reflect the buying public's demands. Along with the introduction of the GT package, March of 1965 saw the introduction of the interior decor group, now affectionately referred to as the "pony interior."

Seat belts on the early cars, 1964½ (right) through early 1965 models, featured rather Spartan chrome latches (actually straight from the Falcon parts bin), while later 1965 (far right) and 1966 models sported latches that corresponded to the seat belt webbing color. Note the design change as well.

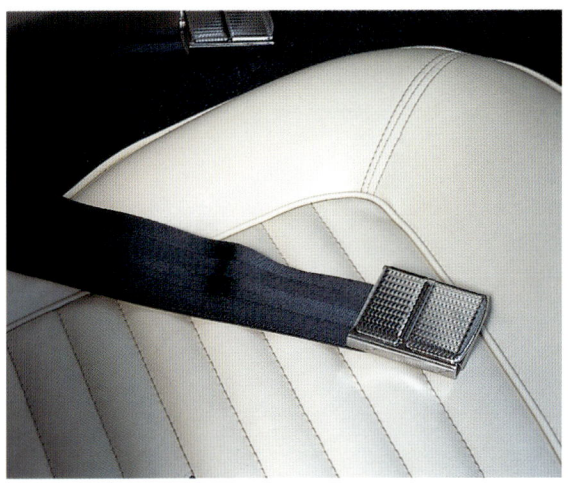

Subtle interior differences included seat belts that secured to the floor with a clasp-type latch and an eyebolt on the 1964½ (above). The 1965 and 1966 (right) cars used a one-piece latch secured with a hex-head machine bolt. Another difference for those with sharp eyes was carpeting on the early cars that stopped at the inner rocker panel, whereas the carpet on the 1965 and 1966 Mustangs was fitted up and over the inner rockers and then secured by the sill plate.

The early Mustangs (far left) came with a color-keyed rubber heel pad that was machine bonded into the carpet. The later 1965 and 1966 (left) models featured a bonded toe pad as well.

Just a couple of basic AM radios you say? Look closer and you'll see that the 1964½'s (left) lowest band number was 600. From the introduction of the 1965 (right) model and up, the lowest band was 500.

Inner door handles and window cranks varied from year to year as well. The early cars (above left) featured door handles and window cranks fastened with a spring-type clip. Once the 1965 model production started (above), the basic design shape changed and the handles and cranks were fastened with Allen-head screws. In March 1965, the interior decor group was introduced. With it came the famed "pistol grip" inner door handles. The option package carried over through the 1966 model year (left).

On the 1964½ cars (far left), door lock knobs were molded plastic and were color-keyed to match the interior. On 1965 and 1966 Mustangs (left), the knobs were reshaped and downsized slightly. They were also chrome plated regardless of the interior color. Subtle changes to the armrest bases were also made. On the 1964½ cars, the inside of the chrome-plated armrest bases were squared off (above left). Look closely, and you'll spot the 1965 and up change (above): the edges were beveled to soften the appearance and to prevent knuckle scrapes.

Under the Hood

The major differences between the model years were engine color and displacement (as identified in chapter 1). As the 1964½ model year got underway, the Mustang utilized Falcon engines (170-ci six-cylinder and 260-ci V-8) as well as the 289-ci V-8. Both the 1965 and 1966 models were distinguished by coloration of engine blocks, valve covers, and air cleaners.

Many smaller changes, however, took place as production moved forward.

The 1964½ Mustangs were equipped with a generator charging system on both V-8 (above) and six-cylinder cars (left). The 1965 and 1966 models utilized alternators.

The 1964½ cars (left) featured larger frame-mounted horns, while 1965 and 1966 (below) Mustang horns were downsized and mounted at the radiator core support. Also, note the design difference in the adjustable hood stops: 1965 and 1966 cars could be turned by hand (below), while the 1964½ (opposite page, top) had to be adjusted with a screwdriver.

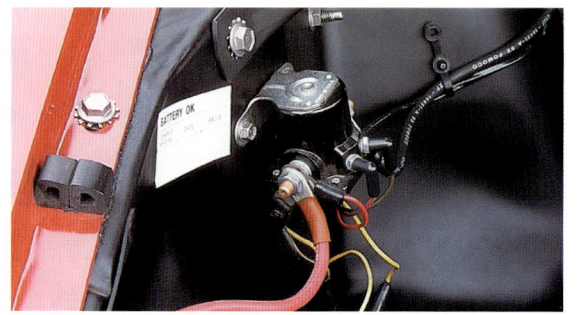

Although they were both FoMoCo parts and basically the same design, the solenoids on 1964½ cars (far left) were molded in a brown textured plastic housing, while later cars (left) went to a solid black color molding.

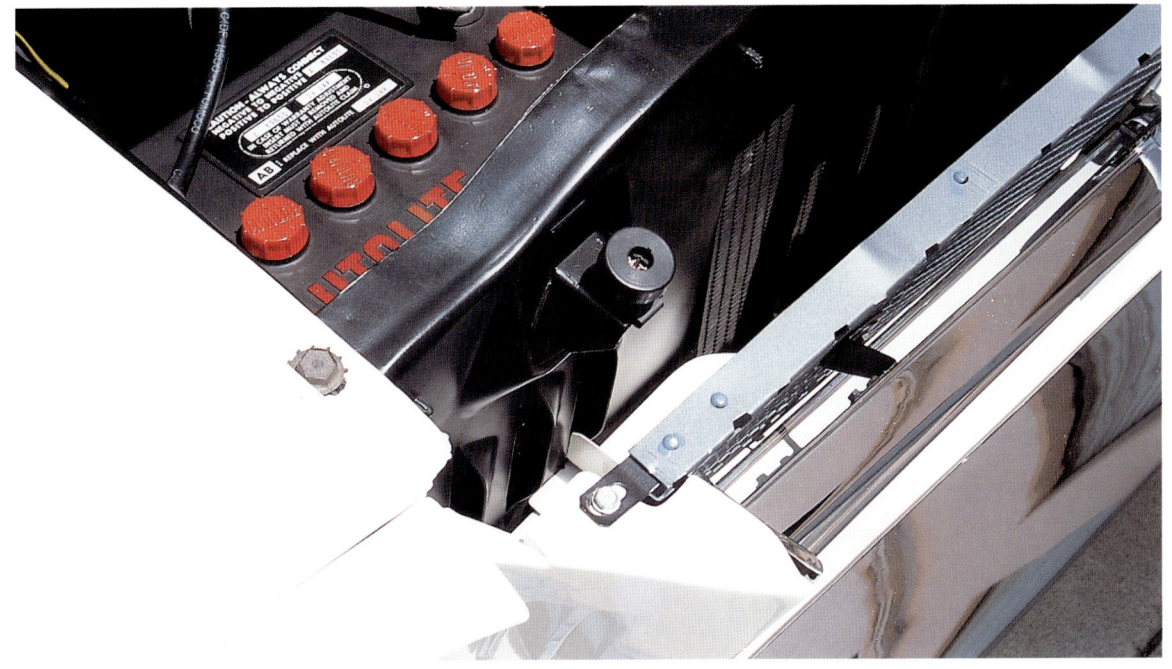

Steel hood hinges on the 1964½ (below left) were painted matte black, while on the 1965 (below right) and 1966 cars they were made from specially treated corrosion-resistant steel and left unpainted.

Master cylinder changes went from a generator charging system on the 1964½ Mustangs (far left) to an alternator on 1965 and 1966 (left) cars. Although not related to the charging system used, the change to alternators moved the cars' brake light switch location. Generator-equipped Mustangs had the brake light switch mounted at the front of the master cylinder.

Chapter 3

1964½

The kickoff was an event of epic proportions. Four days before the Mustang's official unveiling to the general public, proud papa Lee Iacocca played host to 150 reporters and automotive journalists at New York's 1964 World's Fair. After Iacocca whetted their appetites with a full tour of the Ford Pavilion, he treated them to a massive luncheon and proceeded to hand out keys to 75 brand-new Mustangs. Iacocca had it all planned from the beginning. Ever the showman, he then requested that they drive themselves back to Dearborn. What a sure-fire way to get the press on board!

Fast forward three days to April 16, 1964. It's 9:30 P.M., right in the middle of prime time, and the new Mustang debuts simultaneously on all three major television networks. In a series of "infomercial" type airings, more than 29 million viewers caught their first glimpse of Ford's new jewel. The next morning found 2,600 newspapers from around the country saturated with stories and full-page ads. *Time* and *Newsweek* both carried cover stories on the new car in their April 17 editions. The hype worked: an entranced public flocked to Ford dealerships. Mustang Mania had taken hold.

Displayed at banks, shopping centers, hotel lobbies, and convention centers, the new Mustangs became the talk of the town. As television

Above and opposite top: The 1964½ Mustang hardtop in: Wimbledon White (paint code M). Other than the optional wire wheel covers, this car is about as basic as it gets: 170-ci six-cylinder, manually shifted three-speed transmission. Even with a relatively sparse option list, the base Mustangs were real eye-catchers.

The very first hardtop off the Dearborn assembly line was shipped to a dealer in Whitehorse, Yukon Territory, Canada.

The first Mustang out of Dearborn was a Wimbledon White convertible, which now resides in the Henry Ford Museum in Michigan.

and radio commercials continued to bombard the airwaves, Ford Corporate supplied the Indianapolis Motor Speedway with three convertibles to pace the annual Indianapolis 500 race. All the major automotive publications, including *Road & Track, Car and Driver, Car Life, Motor Trend,* and *Popular Hot Rodding* ran full-length features and road tests on the new car.

Part of Ford's marketing strategy was to familiarize everyone in North America with the Mustang. Lee Iacocca was convinced that once people saw the car, they would fall in love with it. And once they realized that it could be had for well under $2,500, they would become serious potential buyers. The well-planned strategy continued to further entice the consumer: full-color, high-gloss sales brochures were liberally handed out in showrooms, and television commercials informed people that they would become exciting, adventure-loving free spirits behind the wheel of a new Mustang. The TV spots featured both men and women, based on market research that indicated the new car appealed equally well to males and females.

The combination of dynamic marketing and the undeniable good looks of the Mustang made for overwhelming success. Almost too much of a success. Even though the Dearborn plant had been producing about 530 Mustangs per day for

six weeks before introduction, it was not nearly enough to satisfy demand. By the close of business on April 17, after just one day of sales, manufacturing was nearly 6,000 units behind! The writing was on the wall: Ford saw its "plight of success," but where could it turn?

Trendsetting California consistently posted the highest sales numbers for new Mustangs at roughly 22 percent. Because the San Jose assembly lines producing Fairlanes and Falcons offered

This Caspian Blue (paint code H), with the interior trim code 82—Blue with Blue Appointments—is the official number 2 car. It spent most of its life on the back roads of Yukon, a northern Canadian territory. Over the next *(continued on next page)*

a facility with a lot of the tooling already in place, Ford took advantage. On June 19, 1964, Ford scheduled a shutdown of the San Jose plant. Fairlane production was shifted to Kansas City, and Falcon manufacturing moved to another Falcon plant in Lorain, Ohio. By July 13, Ford reopened San Jose to work around the clock on its new Mustang line and officially joined Dearborn in the fight to stay on top of it all. Two weeks later, at the end of the day on July 31, the last 1964½

Mustangs rolled off the assembly lines at Dearborn and San Jose. August 1 marked the official start of 1965 model production. All in all, 121,538 Mustangs were produced between March 9 and July 31, 1964.

Although officially coded and titled as a 1965, the first Mustangs were actually introduced as 1964½s. For an incredibly low $2,368, the buyer actually got a lot of automobile. Mustang's list of standard equipment was a real attention grabber:

(continued from previous page) few decades, Mustang went through 14 owners, and finally ended up in Tucumcari, New Mexico. The car's current owner, Bob Fria, purchased it and shipped it back to his home in southern California. After numerous years and a tremendous outlay of cash, this sweet little hardtop looks as good as the day it rolled out of Dearborn.

Standard Equipment
- Front bucket seats
- Sports car steering wheel
- Tunnel-mounted shift lever
- Molded carpets
- Padded instrument panel
- Bright hardware
- Suspended accelerator pedal
- Easy-action convertible top latches (where applicable)
- 16-gallon fuel tank
- Fresh air heater/defroster
- Vinyl upholstery
- Scissors jack
- Rearview mirror
- Aluminum scuff plate
- Extra-wide parallel wipers
- 2-stage door checks

- 2 color-keyed interiors
- Lighter and ashtray
- Courtesy and glove box lights
- Armrests
- Sun visors
- Curved window glass
- Full wheel covers
- Insulated rust-resistant body
- Bolt-on front fenders
- Vinyl headliner
- Counterbalanced hood/deck
- Lid hinges
- Single-action hood latch
- Twice-a-year maintenance
- Bright windshield/backlit molding
- Color-keyed seat belts
- Self-adjusting brakes
- Bear-hug door latches

When the new Mustang was chosen as the official Indianapolis pace car in the spring of 1964, Ford decided to promote the spectacle nationwide. The three actual pace cars were all convertibles, specially equipped with several high-performance options in order to run at sustained high speeds. To commemorate the event, 225 pace car replicas (35 convertibles and 190 hardtops) were built for general public consumption. All the hardtops received the special paint code C, which for 1964½ only represented Pace Car White. Because they weren't assembled in any particular sequential order, the convertible pace car replicas did not receive the C code designation, causing them to lose their pace car status shortly after the big race.

Even though this list of standard goodies was impressive for its day, few cars were actually ordered as "base" models. Dealers pitched the Mustang as "the car that was designed to be designed by you," and indeed it was. Buyers could mix and match options on the car to their heart's content, and most did. More than half of all Mustangs sold were ordered with automatic transmissions, 85 percent were spec'd out with white sidewall tires, 80 percent had radios added, and almost three-quarters of the buying public opted for V-8 power. In fact, the majority of new Mustang owners paid well over $3,000 for their cars; a far cry from the base sticker of $2,368!

Body and Exterior Trim

Initially, Mustangs were only offered as coupes or convertibles. Not until late summer of 1964 (after the 1964½ cars became 1965s) did the sleek 2+2 models appear. With the car's obvious good looks, it almost seemed redundant to actually describe the car. Ford's early sales brochures did a pretty good job: "The front view of Mustang presents a

The hardtop pace car replicas were all equipped with the 260 V-8 engine, automatic transmission, power steering, and standard trim code 42 interior (white with blue appointments). The meticulously restored example shown here sports the correct replica decal stripes and lettering, as well as the "delete" outside rearview mirror. Note the license plate switch from INDY 64 to 64 INDY.

WARRANTY PLATE DECODING FOR 1964½

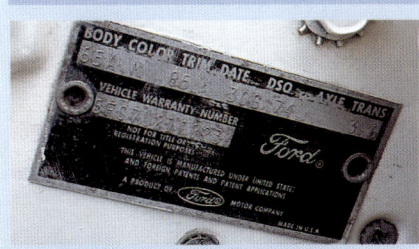

ON THE VEHICLE WARRANTY NUMBER:

Assembly Plant Codes
F = Dearborn, MI (Starting March 9, 1964)
R = San Jose, CA (Starting July 13, 1964)

Body Serial Codes
07 = Hardtop Coupe
08 = Convertible

Engine Codes
D = 289-4V V-8 Low Compression/Regular
   Fuel/Hydraulic Lifter
F = 260-2V V-8 Low Compression/Regular
   Fuel/Hydraulic Lifter
K = 289-4V V-8 High Performance/Premium
   Fuel/Mechanical Lifter
U = 170-1V Six Low Compression/Regular
   Fuel/Hydraulic Lifter

Consecutive Unit Number
The remaining six digits in the VIN indicate the
vehicle's consecutive unit number assigned at the
production line.

ON THE LINE ABOVE THE VEHICLE WARRANTY NUMBER:

Body Style Codes
65A = Hardtop/Standard Interior
76A = Convertible/Standard Interior

Color Codes
A = Raven Black
B = Pagoda Green
C = Pace Car White
D = Dynasty Green
F = Guardsman Blue
H = Caspian Blue
I = Champagne Beige
J = Rangoon Red
K = Silver Smoke Grey
M = Wimbledon White
O = Tropical Turquoise
P = Prairie Bronze
R = Phoenician Yellow
S = Cascade Green
V = Sunlight Yellow
X = Vintage Burgundy
Y = Skylight Blue
Z = Chantilly Beige
3 = Poppy Red

Trim Codes
22 = Blue
25 = Red
26 = Black
42 = White w/Blue Appointments
45 = White w/Red Appointments
46 = White w/Black Appointments
49 = White w/Palomino Appointments
56 = Black w/Cloth
82 = Blue w/Blue Appointments
85 = Red w/Red Appointments
86 = Black w/Black Appointments
89 = Palomino w/Palomino Appointments

Date Codes
C = March 1964
D = April 1964
E = May 1964
F = June 1964
G = July 1964
Note: The number (1–31) that appears before the
month letter indicates the day.

DSO Codes
The warranty plate on every Mustang contained a
DSO code. At the same time the rest of the
individual car's pertinent information was stamped
into its warranty plate, so was the car's specific
end destination. A District Sales Office code
indicates which area of the country that particular
Mustang would be shipped to.

11 = Boston
12 = Buffalo
13 = New York
14 = Pittsburgh
15 = Newark
21 = Atlanta
22 = Charlotte
23 = Philadelphia
24 = Jacksonville
25 = Richmond
26 = Washington, D.C.
31 = Cincinnati
32 = Cleveland
33 = Detroit
34 = Indianapolis
35 = Lansing
36 = Louisville
41 = Chicago
42 = Fargo
43 = Rockford
44 = Twin Cities
45 = Davenport
51 = Denver
52 = Des Moines
53 = Kansas City
54 = Omaha
55 = St. Louis
61 = Dallas
62 = Houston
63 = Memphis
64 = New Orleans
65 = Oklahoma City
71 = Los Angeles
72 = San Jose
73 = Salt Lake City
74 = Seattle
75 = Phoenix
81 = Ford of Canada
83 = U.S. Government
84 = Home Office Reserve
85 = American Red Cross
89 = Transportation Services
90 – 99 = Export

Axle Codes

CONVENTIONAL	LIMITED SLIP	AXLE RATIO
1	A	3.00:1
2	B	2.83:1
3	C	3.20:1
5	E	3.50:1
6	F	2.80:1
8	H	3.89:1
9	I	4.11:1

Transmission Codes
1 = Three-Speed Manual
5 = Four-Speed Manual
6 = C-4 Dual-Range Cruise-O-Matic
F = C-4 Dual-Range Cruise-O-Matic (Canadian expt)

BODY SPECIFICATIONS

	Hardtop	Convertible
Length (overall)	181.6 "	181.6 "
Width (overall)	68.2 "	68.2 "
Height (overall)	51.1 "	51.0 "
Wheelbase	108.0 "	108.0 "
Curb weight (Six-cyl., std. trans.)	2,610 lbs.	2,770 lbs.

honeycomb grille in gunmetal gray with the Mustang emblem in a bright metal rectangle at the center. The rectangle is accented by bright spears on all sides. The grille extends the sweep of the hood ahead of the single-mounted 7-inch headlamps. Small scoop lines in the sheet metal at either side emphasize the forward thrust of the grille . . .

"The windshield is raked 52½ degrees in a true sports fashion, and the curvature of the glass is held to a minimum for a more distortion-free view of the road ahead. Curved, solid tempered safety glass is used for the vent, door, and quarter windows. All side windows are trimmed in bright metal, and the hardtop model features a bright roof drip molding.

"The low center of gravity of the Mustang presents a low-profile view with the look of performance; and the long thrusting hood and extremely compact rear deck both have a short overhang which further suggests sports car design.

"The length of the hood is accentuated by a sculptured area with a sharp sheet-metal edge running from the top of the fender to the quarter panel, then returning to the fender behind the front wheel opening. A bright applique is used at the rear of the sculptured area to simulate an air intake scoop . . .

"The rear view of Mustang presents a wide and clean appearance with a integrated bumper that curves upward at the outer edges to meet the sheet metal. Center fuel filling is standard, and the gas filler tube is covered by a bright, enamel-accented screw-on cap with Mustang identification. Vertical, three-sectional taillights/turn signals are located below the deck lid at either side."

Aside from the obvious external differences between the hardtop and convertible, the two body styles sported exactly the same standard exterior trim.

Right from the car's introduction, an optional body side ornamentation package included bright rocker panel moldings and a fine "Tiffany" pin stripe that was painted around the body sculpturing. When this option was specified, the chrome "scoop" on the rear quarter panel was deleted.

With the same basic design and platform, the exterior dimensions of the hardtop and convertible Mustangs were almost identical.

Above: The base 1964½ interior is trimmed in 85 (red with red appointments). The carpeting shows a toe pad in addition to the rubber heel pad, which is incorrect for 1964½. Toe pads were introduced into the official 1965 production. Below left: All Mustang hardtops received white headlining and sun visors to "enhance the spaciousness of the Mustang's interior." It obviously saved on production costs as well. Below right: Interior door panels were clean and uncluttered. The vertical pleat pattern continued throughout the 1965 production model year.

Above: The early instrument panels carried over into 1965 production, but without the Generator light. Above right: Optional early style Rally-Pac gauges consisted of a tachometer and clock. They were available on any model Mustang, six- or eight-cylinders. The high-performance K-code 289 cars received 8,000-rpm tachs, while all others used a 6,000-rpm unit. Below: Early cars received an adjustable driver's seat with 4½ inches of travel, but the passenger seat remained in a fixed position. Once the 1965 model production was underway, all Mustangs came equipped with adjustable passenger seats. Right: All Mustang instrument panels and glove box doors received the "camera case" black textured finish. The pace car replica shown here was no exception.

Right: All transmission shifters (manual and automatic) were located in the center of the transmission hump just in front of the bucket seats. Far right: Fresh air vents were actuated with a vent knob that contained the letter A for air. Later production knobs were simply black.

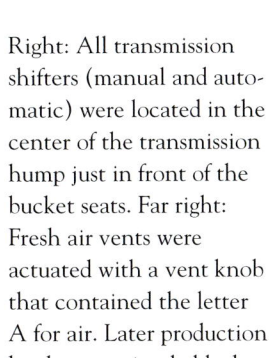

On the inside edge of the driver's door, the vehicle's warranty plate was affixed at the time of the car's assembly. This plate contained all of the pertinent information relating to that particular Mustang.

Interior

With the rare exception of a bench seat–equipped car (introduced on 1965 models), all Mustang interiors from their 1964½ introduction through the 1966 production year were of identical configuration: two bucket seats, a floor-shifted transmission, and a small, two-passenger rear seat. With the mid-April 1964 introduction of the new cars came Ford's seductive sales pitch: "The interior of the Mustang is styled for sports appeal. The two-plus-two seating arrangement features front bucket seats with foam padded cushions and backs with bright side shields. The seats were specially designed for the Mustang and they are sculptured to provide greater comfort. The sewn-in pleats of the seat inserts also add to the comfort and durability of the all-vinyl covering (vinyl and cord stripe cloth is available in black to the hardtop model). Front seat belts with metal-to-metal attachment are standard equipment. The driver's seat allows a 4½-inch fore and aft manual adjustment, and the front passenger seat is mounted in a fixed position. The bucket-styled, two-place rear seat also has sewn-in pleats for the vinyl or black cord stripe covering of the seat inserts.

"All major items of the Mustang's interior are color-keyed to the wide choice of upholstery colors. The sun visors and the headlining in the hardtop are of white textured vinyl which emphasizes the spaciousness of the interior.

"For added durability and long-lasting excellent appearance, the nylon-rayon deep-pile carpeting of the Mustang is molded to the contour of the floor. Bright aluminum scuff plates are used at the door lower body sill to enrich the appearance of the door opening.

"Door upper and lower inner panels are color-keyed textured steel, and a vinyl-covered trim panel through the midsection of each door is bordered with bright mylar. Armrests are positioned for optimum riding comfort; they are also safety-padded and edged in bright trim.

". . . [T]he instrument cluster features bright bezels around the twin circular dials. A 120-mph speedometer is graduated in 5-mph increments. The instrument cluster and glove box door are accented in a "camera case" black crackle finish. The top and facing edge of the instrument panel (dash pad) are safety padded as standard equipment.

"When the optional full-length console is specified, the gear shift selector lever extends through the console. All other applications (automatic or manual shift) are floor mounted at the tunnel."

Convertible Mustangs featured a manually operated top that was designed with counterbalanced springs, providing easy operation of the relatively lightweight roof. An "electro hydraulic" power–operated top was optional.

Chassis

As described in chapter 1, both the hardtop and convertible Mustangs were based on a platform-type chassis. Carried over from the Falcon line, the chassis consisted of boxed front and rear side rails tied into heavily boxed rocker panels. Five heavy-gauge cross-members connected the platform sections together, forming a rigid ladder-type frame. The floor pan was then welded to the front and rear side rails. The full-length transmission/driveshaft tunnel incorporated in the floor pan gave the structure maximum stiffness and rigidity. The engine compartment also added strength, with full-depth side panels (inner fender wells) that were welded to the front side rails and to the cowl area.

These photos depict the convertible's reinforcement points. This particular car is a 1966 Mustang, however the chassis design was identical to the earlier cars.

All convertibles manufactured from the 1964½ intro date through the 1966 model year received extra tubular steel reinforcing bars that were bolted in position at the cowl area and the inner fender well. The car shown is a 1966 model.

Engines

170-1V (One Venturi)

The 1964½ Mustangs were introduced with the 170-ci inline six-cylinder engine as standard equipment. The 170 actually started out in 1960 as a 144, designed exclusively for the Ford Falcon. Over the next couple of years, as demand for power grew, the 144 was increased to 170 cubic inches. Because much of the Mustang's underpinnings were based on the Falcon, it only made sense (technically and financially) to utilize that car's base engine as well. Early Mustang sales brochures praised its base powerplant in 1964: "Ideally suited to Mustang's size and weight, the 170-ci six-cylinder is better-built by Ford to give many thousands of miles of dependable, trouble-free service. The gas-saving-ist of all Mustang engines, this standard equipment powerplant provides sufficient power and performance to meet the needs of most motorists—for both city and country driving."

The narrative went on to describe the 170's bulletproof design: "Construction features include precision-molded castings; a technique that was pioneered and perfected by Ford. This provides maximum strength castings with minimum weight. Both the cylinder block and head are manufactured with this technique, and the savings in weight means extra performance and mileage for Mustang owners, without sacrificing any of the famous Ford reliability. This engine also includes an automatic choke to help provide quicker, more consistent starts in hot as well as cold weather. In addition, greater choke sensitivity is afforded by an engine-to-heater coolant line that is routed next to the choke housing. During partial engine cool-down, the heat from the coolant affects the choke bi-metal spring, preventing full-choking action and thus helping to eliminate flooding and poor economy."

Due to the absence of a solid roof, convertible Mustangs were equipped with "torque boxes" to reinforce and stiffen their chassis. These heavy-duty steel subassemblies were welded to the frame at the cowl area, providing cross-directional rigidity and added strength. Additional chassis rigidity was achieved by a heavy-duty steel plate connected to reinforced sections of the floor pans.

Regardless of engine size (six or eight cylinders), all Mustangs were based on the same platform chassis. Ford relied on an upgraded suspension to compensate for the weight and power differences inherent with the optional V-8 engines.

continued on page 51

BASE EQUIPMENT ENGINE: U-CODE

Type:	Six-cylinder, inline, overhead valve
Displacement:	170 cubic inches
Foundry group:	Falcon "Six"
Bore and stroke:	3.50x2.94
Maximum compression ratio: (with standard gaskets)	8.7:1
Gross horsepower at 4,400 rpm:	101
Gross torque at 2,400 rpm:	156 ft.-lbs.
Valve lifters:	Hydraulic
Carburetor:	Autolite 1100, 1V
Recommended fuel:	Regular
Emission controls CA only:	N/A
Emission controls 49 states:	N/A
Dimensions:	33"L x 33"W x 28"H
Weight:	345 lbs.

OPTIONAL EQUIPMENT ENGINE: F-CODE

Type:	Eight-cylinder, 90-degree V, overhead valve
Displacement:	260 cubic inches
Foundry group:	Fairlane V8
Bore and stroke:	3.80x2.87
Maximum compression ratio: (with standard gaskets)	8.8:1
Gross horsepower at 4,400 rpm:	164
Gross torque at 2,200 rpm:	258 ft.-lbs.
Valve lifters:	Hydraulic
Carburetor:	Autolite 2100, 2V
Recommended fuel:	Regular
Emission controls CA only:	N/A
Emission controls 49 states:	N/A
Dimensions:	28"L x 25"W x 29"H
Weight:	460 lbs.

Above and left: The base equipment engine for the very first Mustangs the 170-ci inline six-cylinder takes up very little room in the engine compartment compared to the larger V-8 blocks.

Opposite above: The "base" equipment V-8 for 1964½ only—the 260-2V V-8. Opposite below: The 260 featured an Autolite 2100 two-barrel carburetor with an automatic choke.

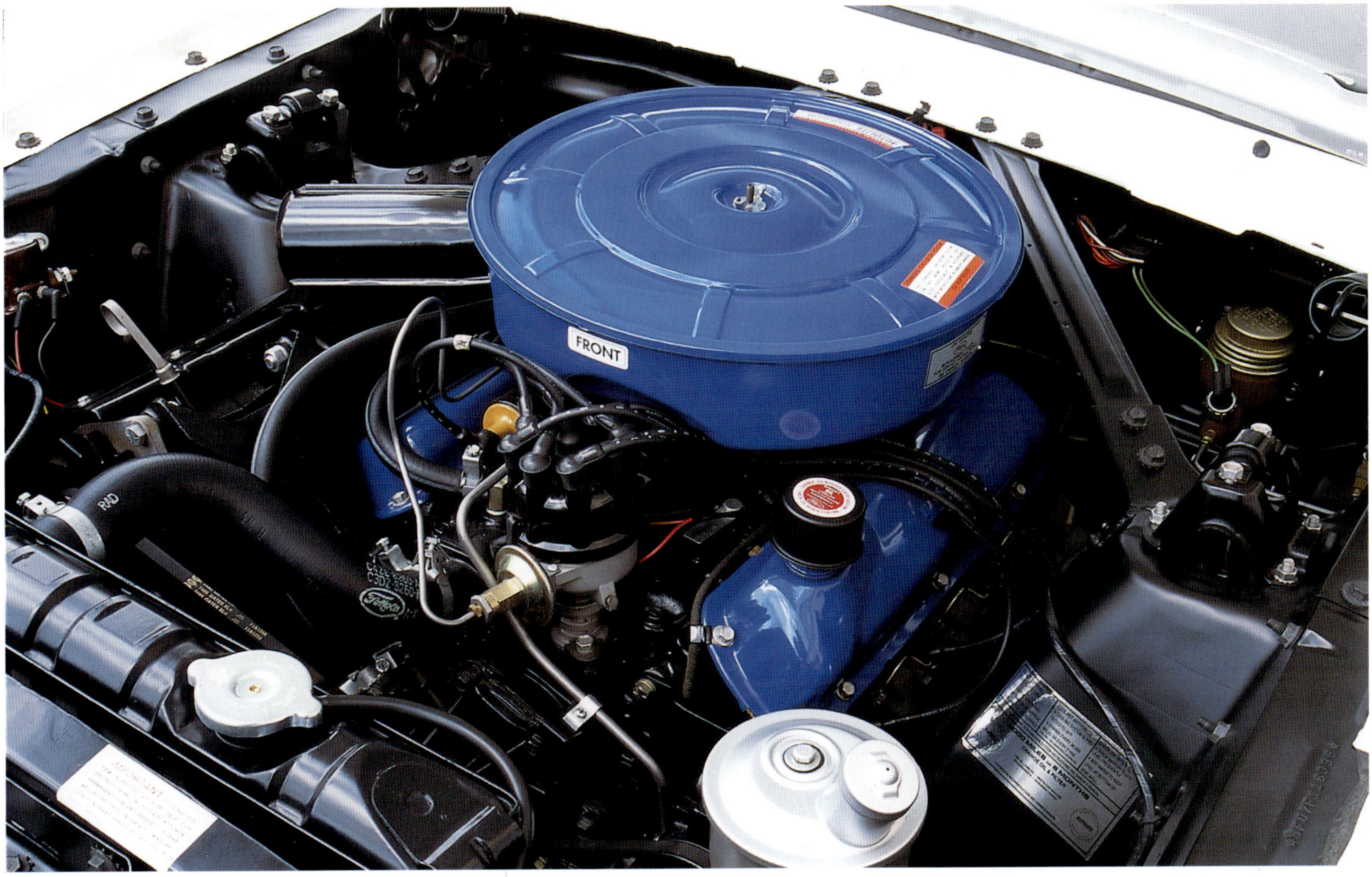
FRONT
RAD

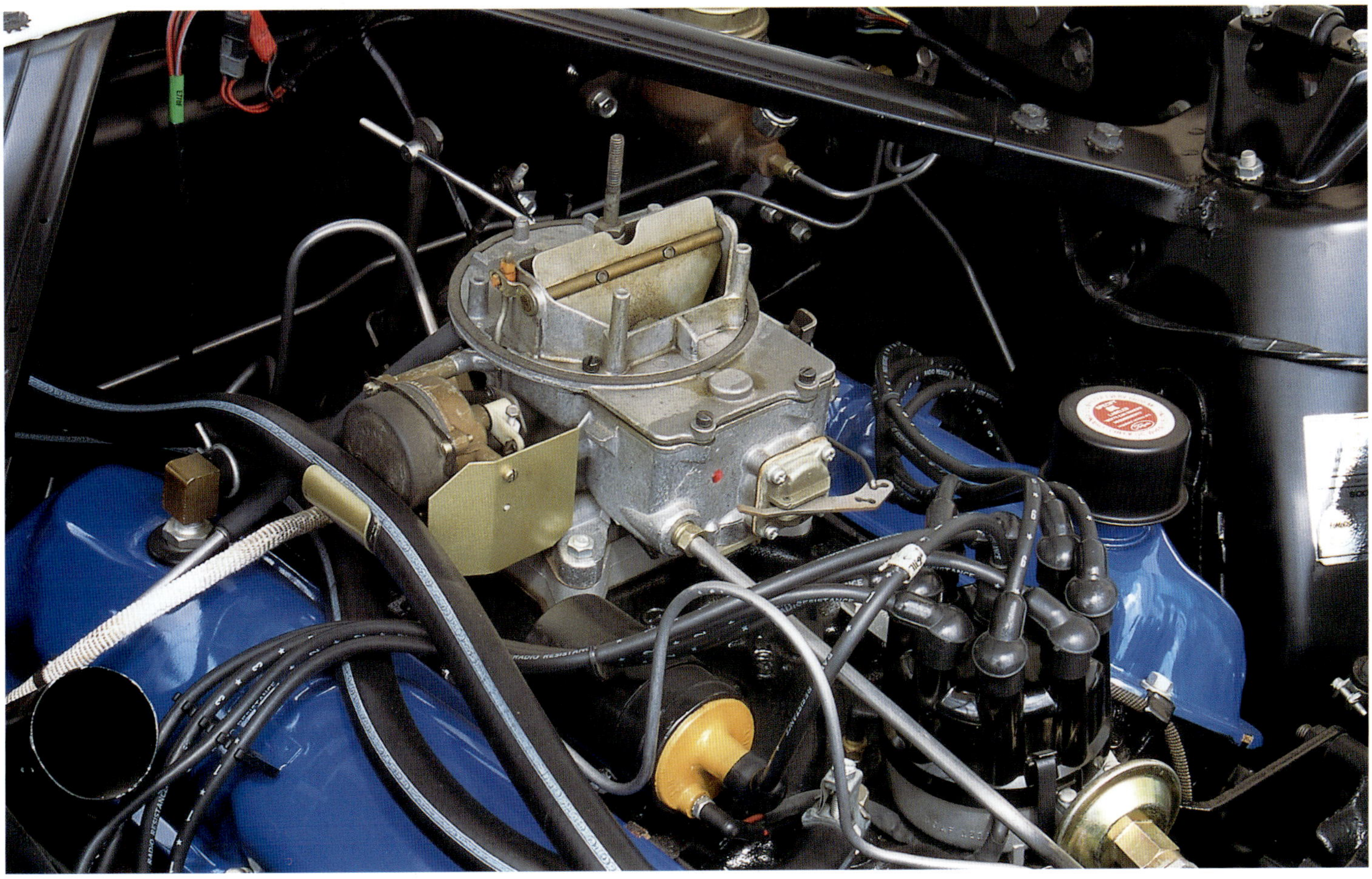

Note the undercoated black chassis and the 260's exhaust system. This 1964½ Mustang was from the Dearborn plant.

The first 289 to appear in a Mustang was the D-code 289 four-barrel. Although it pumped out a healthy 210 horsepower and 300 foot-pounds of torque, with its 9.4:1 rating it was deemed the low-compression 289.

Continued from page 47

As a side note, all 1964½ Mustang engines (including the 170) were equipped with a generator charging system.

(For a complete description of the color schemes associated with 1964½ engines, please see the photos in chapter 1.)

Exhaust

The 170's exhaust system featured a single muffler mounted parallel to, and directly behind, the rear axle. This design allowed Ford to install a 25-inch-long muffler. The extra-long muffler offered less-restrictive airflow and more optimal tuning. Both the muffler and tailpipe were of aluminized construction, and the entire exhaust pipe was a double-wall design.

260-2V

The optional base V-8 for 1964½ was the 260-ci small block, offering 164 horsepower and an impressive 258 foot-pounds of torque. The venerable 260 was first introduced in 1962 as a bored-out version of the new 221: the "Fairlane V-8," as it was dubbed. As the 1963 model year was introduced, Falcons and Comets received the 260 as standard eight-cylinder power (optional over the six-cylinder), while the Fairlane got the 260 only as an option over the 221. Of course, by the time the new Mustang was ready for production, so was the 260.

Thanks to Ford's continued effort at providing commonality among engines, the 1964 version of the 260 was equipped with revised cylinder heads that would accept larger 289 valves. As a result, the heads breathed a little better than the original 260s, but the engine's combustion chamber volume remained unchanged. And although the 1964 260's advertised horsepower wasn't upgraded, it actually did record a few more horses than before. As a side note, 1964 also marked the year the 260 went on to power Carroll Shelby's early AC Cobras, albeit in a highly modified version.

Ford's sales pitch to prospective Mustang buyers was brief and to the point: "The Mustang 260 V-8 is the base optional engine, and with a rating of 164 horsepower it provides over 60 percent more power than the standard 170 Six, while still retaining good economy characteristics. When equipped with the optional Cruise-O-Matic, the 260 V-8 delivers superb motoring pleasure, with excellent performance and maximum driver convenience."

Exhaust

The 260's exhaust system is made up of dual exhaust pipes that connect in a V near where the

OPTIONAL EQUIPMENT ENGINE: D-CODE	
Type:	Eight-cylinder, 90-degree V, overhead valve
Displacement:	289 cubic inches
Foundry group:	Fairlane V-8
Bore and stroke:	4.00x2.87
Maximum compression ratio: (with standard gaskets)	9.4:1
Gross horsepower at 4,400 rpm:	210
Gross torque at 2,800 rpm:	300 ft.-lbs.
Valve lifters:	Hydraulic
Carburetor:	Autolite 4100, 4V
Recommended fuel:	Regular
Emission controls CA only:	N/A
Emission controls 49 states:	N/A
Dimensions:	28"L x 25"W x 29"H
Weight:	465 lbs.

OPTIONAL EQUIPMENT ENGINE: K-CODE	
Type:	Eight-cylinder, 90-degree V, overhead valve
Displacement:	289 cubic inches
Foundry group:	Fairlane V8
Bore and stroke:	4.00x2.87
Maximum compression ratio: (with standard gaskets)	10.5:1
Gross horsepower at 6,000 rpm:	271
Gross torque at 3,400 rpm:	312 ft.-lbs.
Valve lifters:	Solid/adjustable
Carburetor:	Autolite 4100, 4V
Recommended fuel:	Super Premium
Emission controls CA only:	N/A
Emission controls 49 states:	N/A
Dimensions:	28"L x 25"W x 29"H
Weight:	465 lbs.

transmission joins the driveshaft. There the pipes merge into a single pipe that runs the length of the chassis. The pipe then loops over the rear axle and connects to the inlet of a transversely mounted single muffler, which is positioned behind the rear axle in the kick-up area beside the gas tank.

289-4V

Introduced as a V-8 option for 1964½ Mustangs, the base 289 was actually introduced a year earlier, powering Galaxie 500s and XLs. Contrary to popular belief, the 289 was not a bored-out 260. It was a totally new block with much stronger internals. Connecting rods were beefed up in the ribbed neck area and the valve stem diameters significantly increased. Larger ports were used in the intake manifold and the cylinder heads, and the risers to the carburetor were increased to a bigger bore. Valve train changes for the 289 were numerous because springs, retainers, and valve seals were all revised. The new engine's compression ratio of 9.0:1, and its horsepower rating of 195 offered nice improvements over the 260.

By the time the 1964 version of the 289 was introduced, it boasted several improvements over its 1963 predecessor. One of them was an improved PCV system that provided much better ventilation under the valve covers. The big news however, which resulted in a substantial performance gain, was the revised intake manifold and four-barrel carburetor setup. This nice little arrangement, spearheaded by the folks working on the Comet line over at the Mercury division, put out dyno readings that pegged the engine as making 210 horsepower and 300 foot-pounds of torque—perfect for the new ponycar. What's more, the 289's external dimensions were identical to the 260, so fit was not a problem. With all systems go, this motor represented the birth of the fabled small-block Mustang.

A 1964 dealer brochure proclaimed the virtues of the 289: "The largest engine of the lightweight V-8 family, the Mustang 289 V-8 provides additional horsepower with only a fractional increase in weight. As used in the Mustang, the 289 V-8 develops 210 horsepower, and differs from the 260 by having a 4-venturi carburetor, increased compression, greater valve overlap, and larger displacement. Other than these features, the 260 and the 289 V-8 are similar in construction. The 289 V-8 undoubtedly will be the choice of those who want performance to match the sports styling of the Mustang." The pitch went on to further identify the block dimensions of the 260 and the 289, then finished off with ". . . How well this engine concept has succeeded is shown by the adaptation of Ford V-8 engines using this basic block to power European sports cars."

Exhaust

Similar to the 260's exhaust system, the base 289's setup is comprised of dual exhaust pipes that connect in a V near where the transmission joins the driveshaft. There, the dual pipes merge into a single pipe that runs the entire length of the chassis, then loops up and over the rear axle and connects to the inlet of a single muffler. The muffler and corresponding tailpipe are positioned behind the rear axle beside the gas tank.

289-4V "Hi Po"

Available on 1964½ Mustangs in June, the fabled Hi-Performance 289 V-8 literally revolutionized Mustang performance. From that point on, the ponycar had "bite" to back up its bark.

The history of the Hi-Performance 289, affectionately referred to as the "hi-po," began in Ford's Cleveland engine foundry in 1963. Some of the 289 blocks were pulled from the line and checked for lower levels of casting porosity. If no air bubbles or casting flaws were found, heavy-duty main bearing caps were included in the machining process. The "pure" block, align-bored with heavy-duty mains, ended up as the foundation for the "hi-po": a solid, bullet-proof platform strong enough to house all the high-revving mechanicals Ford could throw at it.

The engine's bottom end received a higher-strength, high-nodular cast-iron crankshaft. Specially prepped connecting rods, high-strength aluminum flat-top pistons, special heads with recessed valve spring seats and mechanical lifters mated to a high-lift, long-duration mechanical camshaft rounded out the hi-po basics.

Perched atop the cast-iron 4V intake manifold was an Autolite 4100 four-barrel carburetor with a rating of 480 cubic feet per minute. These carbs were equipped with automatic chokes, and with the exception of some minor calibration and jetting changes, they were similar to the ones used on Galaxie 390 4V engines. Outside air was fed in through an open element air cleaner, while excess gas and air mix was expelled through a set of specially streamlined cast-iron header-type exhaust manifolds.

Externally, the 289 hi-po received chrome valve covers and a chrome-plated air cleaner, further distinguishing it from the base 289. As you can imagine, Ford had plenty to say about its flagship small block in 1964. "For those who will settle for nothing less than top performance, the Mustang is available with Ford Motor Company's lightweight high-performance engine—the 289-ci high-performance V-8. Designed especially for the true sports enthusiast, this powerful V-8 provides sports car performance to match Mustang's sports car styling. Buyers intending to enter competitive events, such as gymkhanas or rallies, will appreciate this engine's breathtaking acceleration—over 600 feet in the first 10 seconds from a standing start." The sales verbiage continued by praising the hi-po's rugged attributes: "A result of Ford's extensive testing and development program—plus further refinements learned from participating in open competition—the 289-ci high-performance V-8 has the reliability and durability to match its high output of 271 horsepower. All engine parts have been thoroughly tested to withstand the extra stresses of high-performance usage. However, durability and reliability have not been accomplished by adding excess weight. This engine is truly a lightweight engine, as evidenced by the extremely favorable power-to-weight ratio of less than 2 pounds per horsepower." Indeed.

Exhaust

The early 289 hi-po's exhaust system was designed to maximize airflow. The engine's individual header-type exhaust manifolds are connected to an H-pipe located near the base of the transmission housing. There, dual exhaust pipes run back along the length of the chassis where they fit into two separate resonators. The pipes then continue up and over the rear axle, and fit into a transversely mounted single muffler. Twin tailpipes leading out of the muffler then exit beneath the rear bumper.

In mid-October of 1964 this exhaust system changed to a more efficient dual muffler setup that is described in detail in chapter 4 . Because 1965 model production started in early August of 1964, this early system found its way onto plenty of early 1965 cars as well.

Transmissions

Both the 170-ci six-cylinder and the base 260-ci V-8 Mustangs came standard with manually shifted three-speed transmissions. There were actually two versions of this transmission: the six-cylinder transmission was synchronized in second and third gears only, while the 260 transmission featured full synchronization in all forward gears.

The conventional three-speed transmission built from cast-iron featured helical-type gears and antifriction bearings for quiet operation and extended life of the transmission. Synchronizers automatically matched the speed of second and third gears to enable relatively quick upshifts and downshifts without gear clash. The downside of a "partially synchronized" transmission was that the car had to be brought to a complete stop before first gear could be selected.

The "constant mesh" three-speed manual

CONVENTIONAL SIX-CYLINDER THREE-SPEED MANUAL GEAR RATIOS

First	3.29:1
Second	1.83:1
Third	1.00:1
Reverse	4.46:1

CONVENTIONAL 260 V-8 CONSTANT MESH THREE-SPEED MANUAL GEAR

First	2.79:1
Second	1.70:1
Third	1.00:1
Reverse	2.87:1

FOUR-SPEED MANUAL TRANSMISSION GEAR RATIOS (SIX-CYLINDER)

First	3.16:1
Second	2.21:1
Third	1.41:1
Fourth	1.00:1
Reverse	3.35:1

FOUR-SPEED MANUAL TRANSMISSION GEAR RATIOS (289-4V AND 289-4V HI-PERFORMANCE)

	289-4V	289-4V "hi-po"
First	2.78:1	2.32:1
Second	1.93:1	1.69:1
Third	1.36:1	1.29:1
Fourth	1.00:1	1.00:1
Reverse	2.78:1	2.32:1

CRUISE-O-MATIC GEAR RATIOS (ALL ENGINES EXCEPT 289-4V HI-PERFORMACE)

First		2.46:1
Second		1.46:1
Third		1.00:1
Reverse		2.20:1
Converter Ratio:	six-cyl.	2.40:1
	eight-cyl.	2.05:1

AXLE BUILD TAGS

All Mustangs carried an ID tag on the differential housing at the point of assembly. In chapter 1, we briefly covered how to decode the information on an axle build tag. The following table further identifies the differential type and the unit's application.
Note: "Equa lock" refers to a limited slip–type differential.

TAG #	DIAMETER	RATIO	TYPE	APPLICATION NOTES
1964½–1965				
WCY-E	7.25"	3.20	Conventional, 2 pin	
WCY-F	7.25"	3.50	Conventional, 2 pin	With manual transmission only
WCY-L	7.25"	3.20	Equa lock, 2 pin	
WCY-N	7.25"	2.83	Conventional, 2 pin	With manual transmission only
WCY-R	7.25"	2.83	Conventional, 2 pin	With automatic transmission only
WCY-AA	7.25"	2.83	Equa lock, 2 pin	
WCY-AJ	7.25"	3.20	Conventional, 2 pin	
WCZ-E	8.00"	2.80	Conventional, 2 pin	With 289-2V
WCZ-F	8.00"	3.00	Conventional, 2 pin	With 289-4V and three-speed manual or auto
WCZ-G	8.00"	3.50	Conventional, 2 pin	With 289-4V and four-speed
WCZ-H	8.75"	3.89	Conventional, 2 pin	With 289 K and four-speed
WCZ-J	8.75"	4.11	Conventional, 2 pin	With 289 K and four-speed
WCZ-P	8.75"	3.50	Conventional, 2 pin	High-performance applications only
WDJ-B	7.75"	2.80	Equa lock, 2 pin	
WDJ-C	8.00"	3.00	Equa lock, 2 pin	289-4V with all transmission types
WDJ-E	8.00"	3.50	Equa lock, 2 pin	289 K and four-speed

transmission was a fully synchronized unit featuring the same cast-iron housing and helical-type gears as the conventional three-speed. All forward gears were in a constant mesh, allowing upshifts and downshifts into any gear without gear clash or the need to double-clutch.

An optional four-speed manually shifted transmission offered specifically for the 170-ci six-cylinder, with gear ratios specifically designed for that engine's torque. It featured full synchronization in all forward gears. Ford described it this way: "This transmission is better built by Ford to provide maximum dependability and more maintenance-free operation. It features a precision cast-iron case for lightness and strength; helical cut gears for quiet, more trouble-free operation; and all antifriction bearings for longer life."

If your Mustang was equipped with either the 289-4V or the 289-4V Hi-Performance V-8, you could order the optional four-speed Top Loader manual transmission designed specifically for those applications. Although available in other Ford vehicles utilizing the 260-2V, this transmission was not available with 260-powered Mustangs.

Ford's sales literature read: "This transmission is designed for engines with much higher output than those used on the Mustang, thus providing an extra measure of strength and dependability for Mustang owners."

Mustangs could also be ordered with the optional Cruise-O-Matic, a three-speed automatic transmission featuring an all-aluminum housing. The only model exempt from this option was the high-performance K-code. Sales literature described the Cruise-O-Matic in 1964: ". . . [T]his top quality automatic combines the latest perfor-

Every Mustang has a rear axle build tag applied at the factory to identify the axle's application, final drive ratio, date of manufacture, and plant code. In this particular case, the code stamping reads WCZ-F 3.00 4DC 901, which translates as follows: WCZ-F = 8" diameter; 3.00 = the final drive ratio of 3.00:1; 4 = 1964; D = April; C = third week (indicating an early build date); 901 = the plant code for Dearborn, Michigan, cars.

mance and convenience features—torque converter starts . . . three forward gear ratios . . . two driving ranges . . . vacuum-operated throttle valve . . . floor-mounted "T" handle gear selector . . . and positive parking lock."

Clutches

On Mustangs equipped with six-cylinder engines, the standard clutch was of a noncentrifugal design. This system uses heavy-duty coil springs behind the pressure plate to maintain engagement.

Both six- and eight-cylinder cars featured a basic upper and lower control arm/coil spring/shock absorber–based front suspension. Six-cylinder cars came with a four-lug wheel (above) while eight-cylinder Mustangs featured a five-lug pattern (right). Both of these cars were equipped with standard drum brakes. The four-lug shown features an original brake drum; the five-lug drum is a reproduction.

On cars that were V-8 equipped, the clutch was based on a semicentrifugal design. Weighted levers, as well as clutch plate springs were used to increase clutch pressure at higher speeds. As the engine speed increased, the clutch plate's gripping power was assisted through centrifugal force.

All clutches on manual transmission Mustangs were a single-disc, dry plate configuration.

Rear Axles

Two different rear axle designs were used in all 1964½–1966 Mustangs: one for six-cylinder applications and another for V-8s. Both axle assemblies were a semifloating hypoid design in which the centerline of the pinion was mounted below the centerline of the ring gear, providing smooth, efficient power output.

Six-Cylinder Models

Cars equipped with the 170-ci six cylinder engine received a rear axle with a differential housing made of cast-iron. This unit was in turn welded to a high-strength steel axle housing, forming a solid, integral assembly. The offset drive pinion was supported by two tapered roller bearings located ahead of the gear. Individual axle shafts were made from induction-hardened steel forgings with cold-rolled splines at the ends that meshed with the differential and wheel hub flanges at the outer ends.

Eight-Cylinder Models

Mustangs equipped with one of the optional eight-cylinder engines utilized a rear axle with a straddle-mounted pinion and a banjo-type housing. The straddle-mounted design gave bearing support on both sides of the pinion and kept the pinion and ring gear in perfect alignment. V-8 differentials were designed with two tapered roller bearings located ahead of the pinion gear and a straight roller bearing behind the gear supporting the pinion shaft, both in front and behind. The axles themselves were made from induction-hardened steel forgings with cold-rolled splines that connected with the differential and wheel hub flanges at the outer ends.

Driveshaft and Universal Joints

All Mustangs featured an exposed driveshaft with universal joints at either end. The driveshafts were manufactured using seamless steel tubing that provided maximum strength and minimum additional weight. Forged yokes were welded on at both ends, then the entire unit was precision balanced.

Universal joints were the cross-and-yoke type that featured sealed, prelubricated needle

SUSPENSION SPECIFICATIONS

Front

Type:	Independent with ball joints
Springs:	4" ID Helical coil, rubber insulated
Shock absorbers:	Hydraulic, telescopic, vertical-mount
Stabilizer:	Link-type, rubber bushings
Steering knuckle:	Integral spindle and spindle support
Wheel bearings:	Opposed tapered roller

Rear

Type:	Variable rate, longitudinal semi-elliptic leaf springs with rubber bushed hangers
Number of leafs:	4
Leaf length and width:	53"x2.5"
Spring shackles:	Compression type, rubber bushings
Shock absorbers:	Hydraulic, telescopic, angle mount

The Bendix-made power steering control valve was a bolt-on on 1964½ cars. Later 1965 control valves were integrated into the tie rod.

bearings. Service was required at 36,000-mile intervals.

Suspension, Steering, Brakes

Although simplistic and typical for its day, the Mustang's suspension system was straightforward and easily serviced. Six-cylinder applications were pulled directly from the Falcon line, while eight-cylinder setups were based on the heavier-duty Fairlane. The front suspension on both six- and eight-cylinder Mustangs utilized independent ball joints, with single lower control arms and upper A-type control arms. They were equipped with independent coil springs, an anti-roll bar, and constant rate shocks.

On both eight- and six-cylinder cars, the rear suspension was identical: The axles were attached to semi-elliptic leaf springs on either side, with each set of springs comprised of four "leafs."

Above: From the Mustang's inception through the 1965 model year, power steering pumps and reservoirs were manufactured by Eaton and FoMoCo.

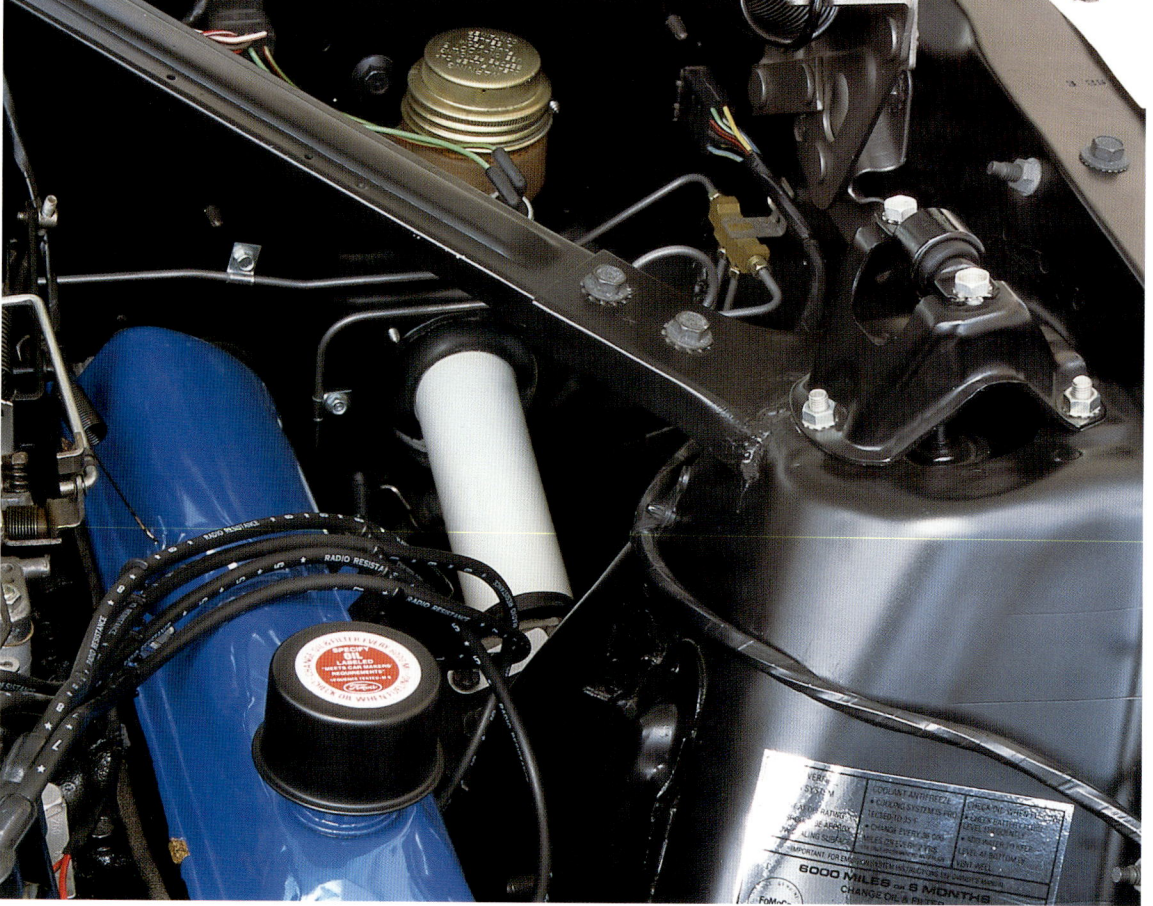

Steering column shafts were painted the same color as the vehicle's exterior—in this instance Pace Car White.

Above: All Mustangs came with a steering box build tag. Above right: Early '64½ master cylinder design changed once into '65 production. The '64½ versions featured a brake light switch that was mounted at the front of the master cylinder.

Springs were calibrated on each car according to the body type (hardtop or convertible) and the vehicle's optional equipment, then bushing-mounted to the frame on the leading end and shackled to the frame rails at the rear. The system was completed with two angle-mounted shock absorbers located just in front of the axle assembly.

On Mustangs equipped with the 289 Hi-Performance V-8, the beefed up suspension system included increased front and rear spring rates: from 89 pounds to 101 pounds, and from 101 pounds to 130 pounds at the rear. Hi-Po cars also received larger front and rear shock absorbers, increased steering ratio (22:1), and a larger front sway bar (increased from .69 inch to .84 inch). This system came optional with the 289-4V engine.

Steering

All Mustangs were equipped with a parallelogram linkage–type steering system. The cross-link and idler arm setup were typical of virtually any American-made automobile. Ford's steering gear was a recirculating ball-and-nut type, identified by the trademark "Magic Circle." All friction points within the entire steering linkage were permanently lubricated. The steering box (and gear) was filled with a life-of-car lubricant.

The optional power steering system, proportional in design, required only 4 pounds of pressure for the steering effort to activate the full power assist. An Eaton-type power steering pump and reservoir were located near the front of the engine compartment, off to the left side of the motor. Several different versions of FoMoCo and Eaton power steering systems were used on 1964½ Mustangs.

STEERING SPECIFICATIONS

Linkage:	Parallelogram with cross-link and idler arm
Gear type:	"Magic Circle" recirculating ball
Overall steering ratio:	
Manual	27:1
Power	22:1
Turns (lock to lock):	
Manual	4.5
Power	3.7
Turning diameter:	38.9 feet
Steering gear box build tags	
1964½	Tag ID
Manual steering (standard):	HCC-AT
Manual steering (performance):	HCC-AX
Power steering:	HCC-AW

The special handling package and the power steering option (by itself) both offered the quicker gear ratio (22:1).

Brakes

All Mustangs, both six- and eight-cylinder models, came from the factory equipped with standard nondisc brakes. The drum design brakes were single-anchor, self-energizing, internal-expanding, and air-cooled. Self-adjusters automatically adjusted the brake linings as required when the brakes were applied while the car was moving in reverse. Guaranteed for the service life of the brake linings, the self-adjusters also helped maintain the proper brake pedal height.

The jar-type cap and diaphragm-type gasket on the hydraulics of the Mustang's braking system sealed it against the outside elements.

FoMoCo-built generators charged Mustangs until the switch to alternators on 1965 models. Shown here are generators from six- and eight-cylinder cars.

The parking/emergency brake, conventional in design, could be engaged by a twist-and-release handle located under the left side of the instrument panel.

Optional front disc brakes could be ordered on 1964½ Mustangs equipped with a V-8 engine. In the traditional fashion, the brakes incorporated a cast-iron disc with a brake pad on either side. Each brake pad was actuated by two brake cylinders. The disc (rotor) was a one-piece casting with radial ribs separating the two sides of the disc, allowing air circulation for maximum heat dissipation. The rear brakes used a conventional drum design.

Power-assisted brakes were also available as an option, but could not be ordered if disc brakes were specified. The vacuum-operated power booster was manufactured by Bendix on all early cars and featured an adjustable pushrod with tolerances between .980 inch and .995 inch.

Brake specifications:

	Six-Cylinder	Eight-Cylinder
Brake drum diameter	9 in.	10 in.
Lining material	Molded asbestos	
Lining attachment	Riveted	
Total lining area (sq. in.)	131.0	154.2

Electrical, Cooling, Heating

The first Mustangs used a belt-driven generator-based charging system that was of the direct current (DC) variety. A 12-volt electrical system was used in conjunction with 25-amp generators on six-cylinder cars, and with 30-amp generators on V-8 Mustangs. Six-cylinder cars also received a 54-plate/40-amp-per-hour battery, while eight-cylinder cars were equipped with a 55-amp/hour-based 54-plate battery.

Two radiator models were used on 1964½ Mustangs: six-cylinder cars used an 8½-quart capacity unit, V-8 powered cars received 14-quart versions. Both radiators were fully pressurized and thermostatically controlled. Thermostats were located at the upper engine outlet on both six- and eight-cylinder engines.

Fan blades vary widely depending on the particular car's optional equipment and its build date. On the early cars equipped with air conditioning units, a six-bladed fan was affixed to a cast-iron engine pulley. Cars built during the changeover to the 1965 model year that were a/c optioned had five-bladed fans that mounted to a stamped-steel engine pulley. Mustangs not equipped with air conditioning used four-bladed fans.

Optional air conditioning units produced by Ford were mounted directly under the center of the instrument panel. On 1964½ and 1965 a/c units, the face was painted dull silver and featured four circular bezels to direct airflow. The fan featured three speeds: High (6.5–7.5 amps), Medium (4.5–5.5 amps), and Low (3–4 amps). All air conditioner compressors were located near the front of the engine and were typical belt-driven units. A 3AG 15-amp fuse provided circuit protection.

Early Mustang heaters were located underneath the passenger side of the instrument panel and used water circulated and heated from the engine to operate. The blower motor could be operated at two different fan speeds: High produced a 6–8 ampere draw, while Low drew 2–4 amps. The

Early FoMoCo voltage regulators were larger models than those associated with the alternator charging system.

1964½ Mustangs featured core supports with cooling fins located just in front of the battery that were designed to help maintain air-flow circulation around the battery on generator-charged cars.

Below: An original cap manufactured by Autolite seals an 8½-quart radiator from a six-cylinder car.

heater/blower used a circuit protector with a SFE 14-amp fuse.

Wheels and Tires

With the exception of the K-code cars, the first Mustangs (both six- and eight- cylinder models) were introduced with 13-inch wheels. The "six-cylinder" wheels had a four-lug pattern, while the "V-8" wheels were five-lug. Both styles had a bead width of 4½ inches. Fourteen-inch wheels were optional on both six- and eight-cylinder Mustangs. The special handling package (which included 14-inch wheels and tires as well as a heavy-duty suspension) was optional on all V-8–powered cars, and was standard equipment on 289-4V K-code Mustangs. Up until the fall of 1964, 15-inch wheels could be ordered as an extra cost option, but only on cars equipped with the previously mentioned handling package.

All 1964½ Mustangs (six and eight cylinders) came standard with 6.50"x13" four-ply rayon black sidewall tires. High-grade nylon tires and white sidewall versions were optional on both the 13-inch and 14-inch sizes. The special 15-inch tires were available in 5.70" and 5.90" sizes (only on handling package–equipped cars) but were discontinued

in September of 1964 in favor of the new dual red line 14-inch nylon tires. The new dual red line rubber was offered as standard equipment on the K-code cars, and was optional on all other Mustangs equipped with V-8 engines. Eight-cylinder cars with air conditioning received the 6.95"x13" tires as standard equipment.

All 13-inch and 14-inch tires were available with white sidewalls.

WHEEL SPECIFICATIONS

	Six-Cylinder	Eight-Cylinder
Type	Stamped-steel ventilated disc with safety-type rims	
Number of studs	4	5
Diameter and rim size:		
Standard	13"x4.5"	13"x4.5"
Optional	14"x4.5"	14"x5"
		15"x5.0"

TIRE SPECIFICATIONS

	6.50" x13"	6.95" x13"	6.50" x14"	5.60"/ 5.90"x15"
Six-cyl.	std	-	opt	-
Eight-cyl.	std	opt	opt	-
Eight-cyl.*	-	-	std	opt

*with handling package

Far left: The standard wheel cover for all Mustangs came in 13-inch and 14-inch versions. Left: Optional wheel cover for 13-inch or 14-inch applications featured a knock-off style center cap.

Far left below: Optional wire wheel covers for 14-inch applications included a knock-off-style center cap that extended outward significantly from the body of the car, earning them the nickname "Chariot style." This wheel cover was discontinued due to its inherent safety risks in mid-1964. Left: Optional wire wheel covers for 13-inch or 14-inch applications were similar to the Chariot-style version with the center cap in a more recessed position.

Firestone brand tires were standard fare on all Mustangs.

OPTIONS

The following list of options is taken from early model dealer pricing literature. Even with the very first cars, the choices offered to the public were extraordinary. A Mustang truly was "the car that was designed to be designed by you."

Base Price:
2-Door Hardtop: $2,368.00
Convertible: $2,614.00

Engines:
•Eight-Cylinder 260-CID 2V 164-HP	$75.00
(extra charge over 170-CID 1V 101-HP Six-Cylinder)	
•Eight-Cylinder 289-CID 4V 210-HP	$87.00
(extra charge over 260-CID 2V)	
•Eight-Cylinder 289-CID 4V 271-HP Hi-Performance	$442.60
(extra charge over 260-CID 2V, includes Special Handling Package and 6.95x14 Dual Red Band Nylon Tires)	

Transmissions:
•Cruise-O-Matic Six-Cylinder	$179.80
•Cruise-O-Matic 164/220-HP V-8	$189.60
•Four-Speed Manual Six-Cylinder	$115.90
•Four-Speed Manual V-8	$75.80

Performance Equipment:
•Disc Brakes, Front, Eight-Cyl. (N/A with power brakes)	$58.00
•Limited Slip Differential	$42.50
•Rally Pac (includes Clock/Tachometer)	$70.80
•Special Handling Package, 220-HP V-8 Engines	$31.30
(includes increased-rate front and rear springs, larger front and rear shock absorbers, 22:1 steering ratio, and larger-diameter front stabilizer bar)	
•Wheels, 14-inch Styled Steel (V-8 only)	$122.30

Power Assists:
•Power Brakes	$43.20
•Power Steering	$86.30
•Power Top, Convertible	$54.10

Safety Equipment:
•Emergency Flashers	$19.60
•Padded Visors	$5.70
•Deluxe Front Seat Belts (retractable)	$7.55
•Visibility Group (includes remote-control mirror, day/nite mirror, two-speed electric wipers and washer)	$36.00

Appearance/Comfort Equipment:
•Accent Group (includes body side paint stripe, rocker panel molding, no rear quarter ornamentation)	$27.70
•Air Conditioner (Ford)	$283.20
•Back-Up Lamps	$10.70
•Battery, Heavy-Duty	$7.60
•Closed Emission System (CA only)	$5.30
•Console, Full Length	$51.50
•Console (for use with air conditioner)	$32.20
•Glass, Tinted with Banded Windshield	$30.90

•Windshield Only, Tinted and Banded	$21.55
•Radio, Push Button and Antenna	$58.50
•Rocker Panel Molding	$16.40
•Vinyl Roof	$75.80
•Wheel Covers w/Knock-Off Hubs	$18.20
•Wire Wheel Covers, 14-inch	$45.80
•Magic Aire Heater, Delete (Credit)	($32.20)
•Seat Belts, Delete (Credit)	($11.00)

Optional Tire Prices:
Five 6.50x13 BSW Rayon tires were standard equipment on all six-cylinder models. Extra charge for
•6.50x13 WSW	$33.90
•6.95x14 BSW	$7.40
•6.95x14 WSW	$41.30

Five 6.95x14 BSW tires were standard equipment on all eight-cylinder models except the 271-HP Hi-Performance engine. Extra charge for:
•6.95x14 WSW	$33.90
•6.95x14 BSW Nylon	$15.80
•6.95x14 Dual Red Band, Nylon	$49.60

Dealer-Installed Accessories:
•Door Edge Guards	$2.70
•Rocker Panel Molding (set)	$19.10
•Wheel Covers, Deluxe with Spinner (13 in.)	$28.95
•Wheel Covers, Deluxe with Spinner (14 in.)	$28.95
•Wheel Covers, Simulated Wire (13 in.)	$58.35
•Wheel Covers, Simulated Wire (14 in.)	$58.35
•Luggage Rack	$35.00
•Tonneau Cover (White)	$52.70
•Tonneau Cover (Black)	$52.70
•L.H. Spot Light	$29.95
•Vanity Mirror	$1.95
•License Plate Frame	$4.50
•Fire Extinguisher	$33.70
•Compass	$7.95
•AM Radio	$53.50
•Rear Seat Speaker	$11.95
•Studio Sonic Sound System (Reverb)	$22.95
•Round (Cone-Shaped) Outside Mirror	$3.95
•Left-Hand Remote Mirror	$2.25
•Universal (Flat) Outside Mirror	$12.75
•Matching Right-Hand	$6.95
•Inside Day-Night Mirror	$4.95
•Back-Up Lights	$10.40
•Power Brakes	$47.00
•Glove Box Lock	$2.49
•Remote Control Trunk Release	$6.95
•Windshield Washers	$14.50
•Rally-Pac (Six-cylinder)	$75.95
•Rally-Pac (Eight-cylinder)	$75.95

Chapter 4

1965

According to popular belief, 1965 model production began August 1, 1964, at both the Dearborn and San Jose plants. However, over the years some speculation surrounds the true 1965 model start-up date. Information published in the book *In Search of Mustangs* states that both Dearborn and San Jose produced their final 1964½ cars on the last day of July 1964. But according to early Mustang experts Jim Smart and Jim Haskell, reports of 1964½ cars with scheduled assembly dates in late July and early August of 1964 exist. These Mustangs had sheet metal and various com-

ponents stamped with early- to mid-August date coding. Further digging revealed that although Ford had intended to end 1964½ model production on July 31st, production schedules may have fallen behind, and the actual 1965 start-up date was probably later in August. To cut through any confusion, a simple rule for identifying a true 1965 model can be applied: If it has an alternator and an engine code of either A, C, T, or K, it's a 1965.

The 1965 models came with several major changes. Most notable was the introduction of the fastback body style, the dynamic GT package, and

Above: The new-for-1965 Mustang GT is identified by auxilliary lights set in the grille.

Opposite: Early 1965 production A-code convertible in Poppy Red (paint code 3).

1965 EQUIPMENT

Here's how Mustang's base equipment looked in a 1965 sales brochure:

Standard Equipment
- Air Cleaner Filter: 36,000 miles
- Accelerator Pedal: Suspended Type
- Alternator: 38 amps
- Ash Tray: Front
- Arm Rests: Front
- Arm Rests, Ash Trays: Rear (convertible)
- Body: Rust Resistant
- Brakes: Self-Adjusting
- Bucket Seats: Foam Padded
- Carpets: Nylon; Rayon Molded
- Cigarette Lighter
- Coat Hooks
- Coolant: 2 years or 36,000 miles
- Courtesy Lights: Door Switches
- Curved Side Glass
- Door Checks: Two-Stage
- Door Hinges: Bronze Bushed
- Door Latches: Safety Type
- Door Trim: All Vinyl
- Engine: 200-ci six-cylinder
- Finish: Diamond Lustre Enamel
- Front Fenders: Bolt-On
- Fuel Filter: 36,000 miles
- Fuel Tank: 16 gallons
- Glass: Safety
- Glove Box Light
- Headlining: White Vinyl
- Headlining: Color-Keyed Vinyl (fastback)

- Heater and Defroster: Fresh Air
- Hood Latch: Single Action
- Horns: Dual
- Instrument Panel: Padded
- Insulated Body
- Jack: Scissors Type, Body Side
- Lamp Bulbs: Extended Life
- Lubrication, Chassis: 36,000 miles
- Maintenance: Twice a Year
- Mirror: Inside Rearview
- Molding: Rocker Panel (fastback)
- Muffler: Aluminized
- Oil Filter: 6,000 miles
- Scuff Plates: Aluminum
- Seat Belts: Front
- Seat, Rear: Folding (fastback)
- Steering Wheel: Deep Dish, Safety Type
- Sun Visor: Dual
- Sun Visor: Padded, Color-Keyed (fastback)
- Transmission Lever: Tunnel mounted
- Transmission: Three-Speed Manual
- Turn Signals
- Upholstery: All Vinyl
- Upholstery: Cloth and Vinyl (except convertible)
- Valve Lifters: Hydraulic
- Ventilation: Cowl Aire intakes (except fastback)
- Ventilation: Cowl Aire plus Roof Vent Outlets (fastback)
- Wheel Covers: Full
- Windshield Wipers: 15" Electric

Above and top opposite: This is as good as it gets. The spectacular K-code 1965 GT fastback in paint code A (Raven Black).

GARDEN GROVE
CALIFORNIA
NHE 470
SMITH MOTOR CO.

FORD
GARDEN GROVE
CALIFORNIA
NHE 470
SMITH MOTOR CO.

the change in the charging system from generator to alternator.

It was also the start of the fabled Shelby Mustangs, the introduction of the 200-ci six-cylinder engine (and the end of the 170 and 260) as well as two new versions of the 289-ci V-8. But mostly, 1965 was a year of upgrades.

Mustangs were becoming more sophisticated. In addition to the expanding model line, available options were more exciting than ever. The standard equipment list looked like it had been substantially beefed up (and pulled from a car costing hundreds more). For the asking price, Mustangs were the bargain of the century. Base price of the standard coupe in 1965 was $2,320. The glamorous convertible stickered at $2,557, and the hot new fastbacks were introduced at $2,533.

Ford's ongoing sales pitches and promotions put the public in a buying frenzy. Light-hearted "zero to hero" based ads were designed to convince people that they would actually undergo complete personality transformations behind the wheel of a new Mustang. The ads cleverly voiced the certainty of an improved lifestyle while at the same time pushing the car's impressive list of standard features. In retrospect, the ads reflected typical sixties humor, but the vast majority of viewers bought into the catchy TV and print spots.

"Wolfgang used to give harpsichord recitals for a few close friends. Then he bought a Mustang. Things looked livelier for Wolfgang, surrounded by bucket seats, vinyl interior, padded dash, wall-to-wall carpeting (all standard Mustang) . . . and a big V-8 option that produces some of the most powerful notes this side of Beethoven. What happened? Sudden fame! Fortune! The adulation of millions! Being a Mustanger brought out the wolf in Wolfgang. What could it do for you?"

As in the early campaigns, the ads were geared equally to men and women alike:

"Life was just one diaper after another until Sarah got her new Mustang. Somehow Mustang's sensationally sophisticated looks, its standard equipment luxuries (bucket seats, full carpeting, vinyl interior, chiffon-smooth floor-mounted transmission), made everyday cares fade far, far into the background. Suddenly there was a new gleam in her husband's eye. (For the car? For Sarah? Both?) Now Sarah knows for sure, Mustangers have more fun."

Above and opposite top: A 1965 289 Mustang fastback in Tropical Turquoise (paint code O). *Photo by Tom Shaw*

Opposite: Views of a 1965 289 Mustang hardtop in Silver Smoke Gray (paint code K).

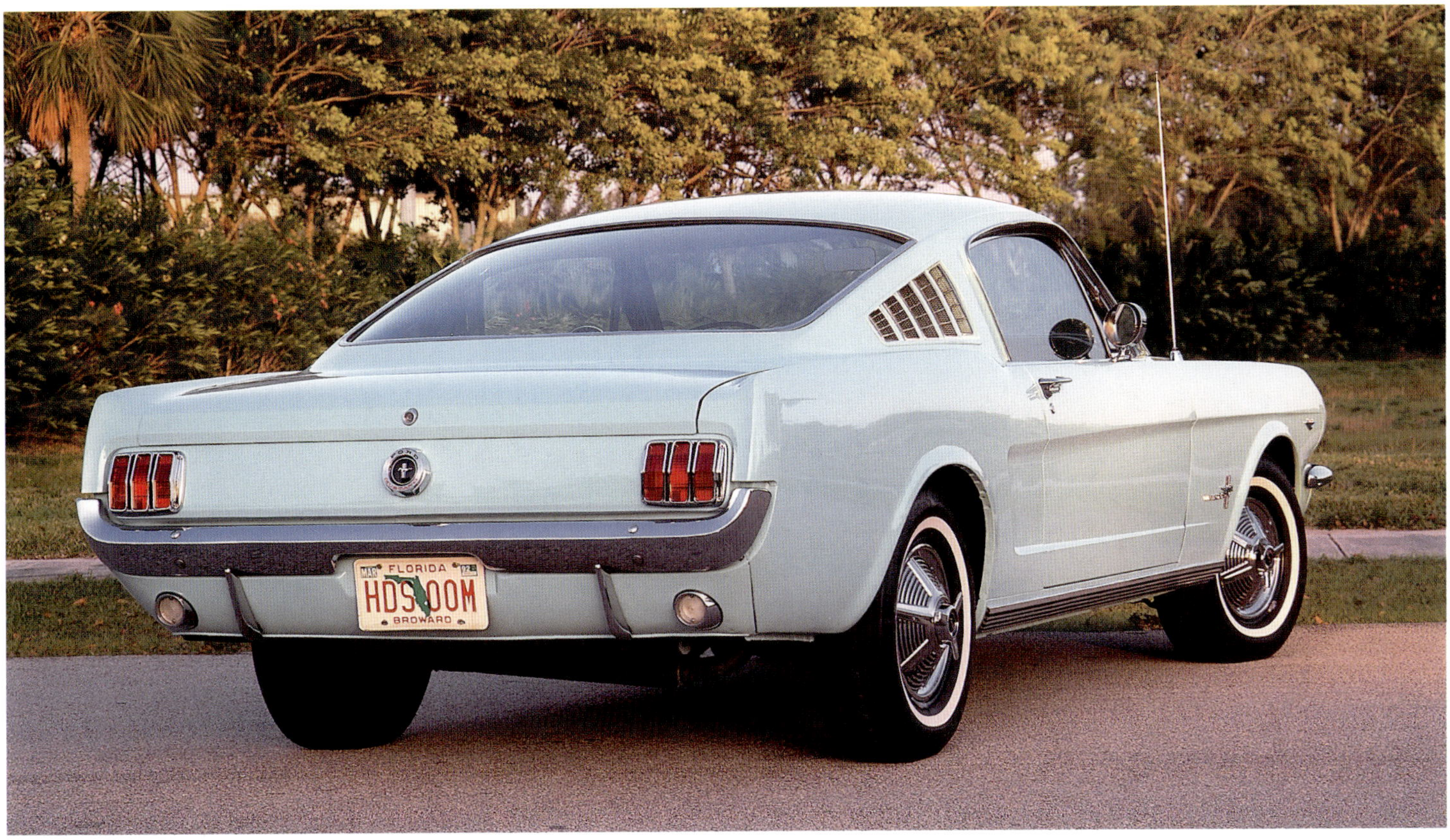
FLORIDA
BROWARD

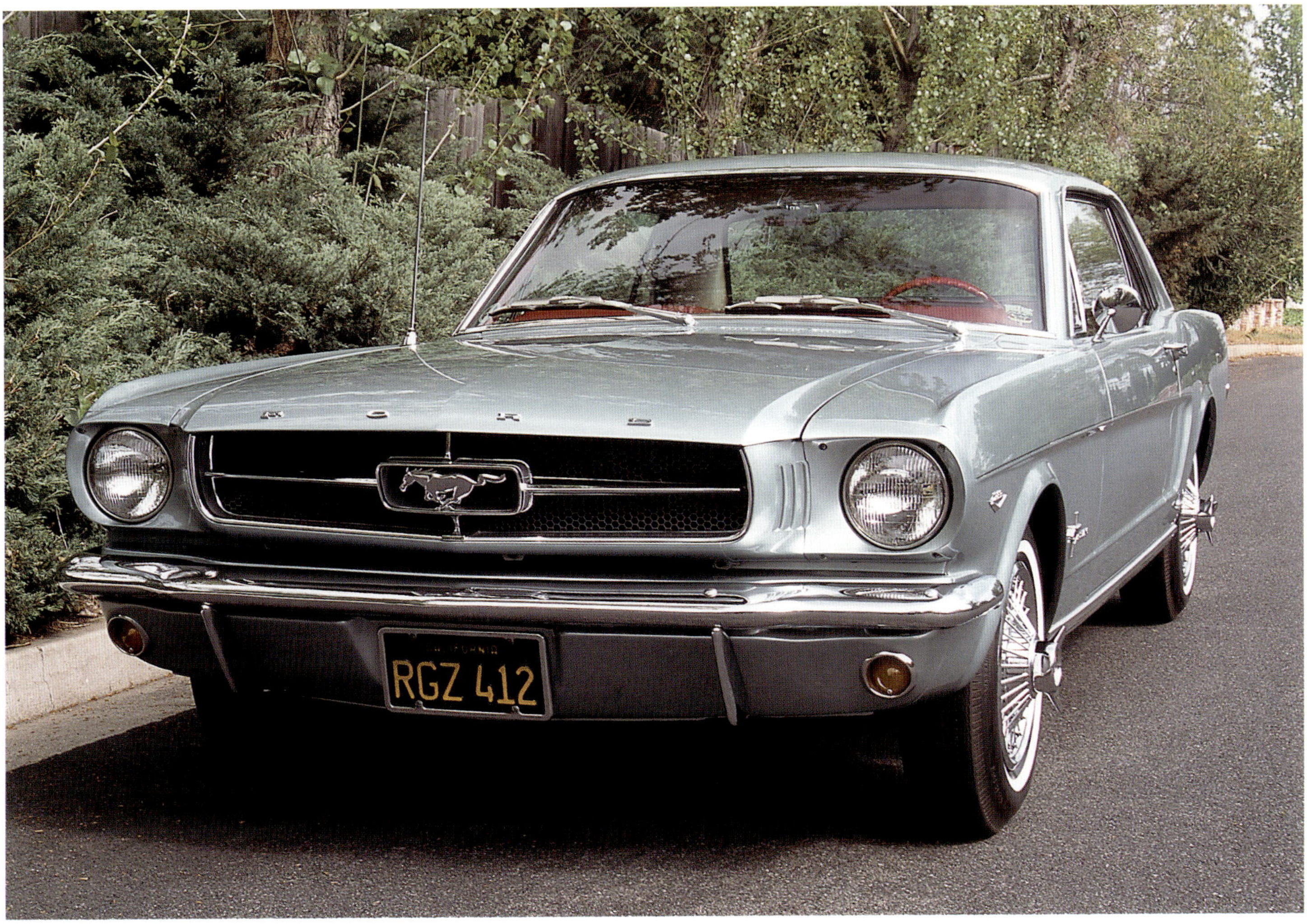
RGZ 412

Not all ads pushed the personality transformation aspects of Mustang ownership. Now that the car was widely regarded as a free-spirited, fun-loving performance automobile, Ford's ad agencies decided to target yet another audience. In a print ad dubbed "The Sweetheart of the Supermarket Set," direct aim was taken at the young woman with a family. The ad pushed the Mustang's "ease of parking, elegance, economy, and room for a bundle of groceries."

With the fastback 2+2 Mustang making its debut in September of 1964 and the introduction of the GTs in the spring of 1965, Ford now boasted a serious high-performance lineup. Along with the new models came advertising with more of an edge. The new slogan was simply "Best year yet to go Ford. Test Drive Total Performance '65." Ads featuring young couples blasting down the highways and byways of America in GT fastbacks were the order of the day. Of course, all this publicity fueled the Mustang fire as it became a national obsession. Although Dearborn was building Mustangs at an incredible rate of 1,320 per day and San Jose was good for 480, orders were still outstripping production. Ford's plant in Metuchen, New Jersey, was about to step up.

During the entire month of January 1965, Metuchen manufacturing moved its Falcon production to Ohio and retooled its facilities for full-time Comet and Mustang assembly. Come February 1, 1965, the revised plant was rolling out its first Mustangs.

By springtime of 1965, Dearborn, San Jose, and Metuchen were finally getting ahead of the curve. For the first time in more than a year Mustangs were now ready for immediate delivery, and the sales numbers just kept climbing. The year 1965 had been a contest between marketing and production, and as a result, 559,451 additional Mustangs were now roaming the streets. August 20 would mark the last official day of 1965 model production at the San Jose plant. Dearborn and Metuchen had phased out production in late July and mid-August, respectively.

Body and Exterior Trim

Aside from the minor exterior detail differences as mentioned in chapter 2, the hardtop and convertible 1965 Mustangs were identical to their earlier counterparts. The big news for 1965 however, was the introduction of the hot new 2+2

65 Fastbacks featured functional venting that sucked air into the cars interior.

Quarter panel simulated air scoop ornamentation was carried over through the 1965 model year.

The optional remote-control mirror added style and convenience. When a right-hand version (passenger side) was also specified, it was of the same design but nonfunctional.

fastbacks. Making their debut on September 9, 1964, they offered a two-passenger car with minimal seating for two additional passengers in the fold-down rear seat. Two-plus-two Mustangs, when equipped with the Hi-Performance K-code engine package, would go on to become the basis for Shelby's famed GT-350.

Although April 1965 is the commonly accepted introduction date of the GT Mustangs, Jim Smart's book, *Mustang Production Guide: 1964½–1966*, notes the appearance of GT-equipped cars as early as late February. A combination performance and appearance package, the GT (Gran Tourismo) equipment group was available on Mustangs specified with either A-code (289-4V) or K-code (289-4V Hi-Performance) engines only. Exterior details on GT-equipped cars were unique: The grille was painted gunmetal gray like standard Mustangs and featured two circular high-intensity fog

lamps that were attached to the horizontal grille bars. A bright metal hood lip molding was standard, as was special GT ornamentation that included fender-mounted emblems and full-length body striping. The quarter panel chrome air scoop molding was deleted on GTs, and the rear bumper guards were removed in favor of chrome "trumpeted" dual exhaust tips that exited through the rear valance.

Although they remained an option on the hardtop and convertible Mustangs, bright rocker panel moldings were offered as standard equipment on the new fastbacks.

Body configuration aside, the hardtop, convertible, and fastback Mustangs all shared the same basic design and platform. Exterior dimensions are listed in the sidebar nearby.

On the inside edge of the driver's door, the vehicle's warranty plate was affixed at the time of the car's assembly. This plate contained all the

WARRANTY PLATE DECODING FOR 1965

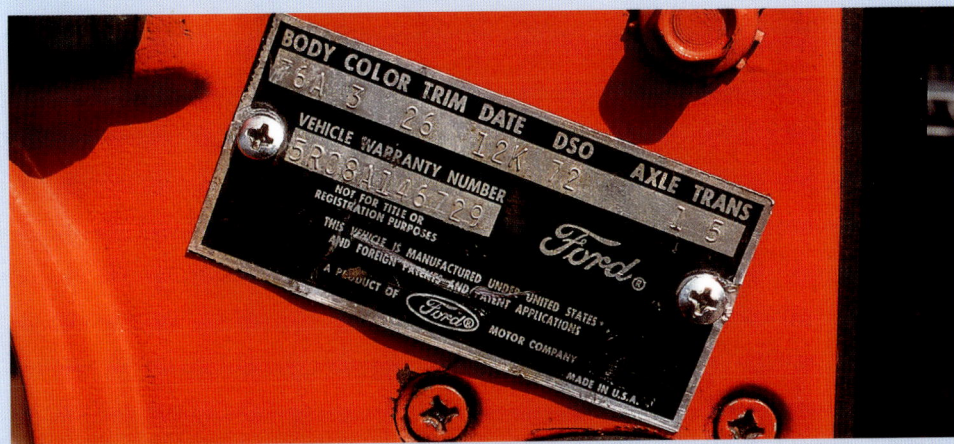

ON THE VEHICLE WARRANTY NUMBER:

Assembly Plant Codes
F = Dearborn, MI
R = San Jose, CA
T = Metuchen, NJ (Starting on February 1, 1965)

Body Serial Codes
07 = Hardtop Coupe
08 = Convertible
09 = Fastback

Engine Codes
A = 289-4V V-8 High Compression/Premium Fuel/Hydraulic Lifter
C = 289-2V V-8 Low Compression/Regular Fuel/Hydraulic Lifter
K = 289-2V V-8 High Performance/Premium Fuel/Mechanical Lifter
T = 200-1V Six Low Compression/Regular Fuel/Hydraulic Lifter

Consecutive Unit Number
The remaining six digits in the VIN indicate the vehicle's consecutive unit number assigned at the production line.

ON THE LINE ABOVE THE VEHICLE WARRANTY NUMBER:

Body Style Codes
63A = Fastback/Standard Interior
65A = Hardtop Coupe/Standard Interior
76A = Convertible/Standard Interior
63B = Fastback/Interior Decor Group (Pony Interior)
65B = Hardtop Coupe/Interior Decor Group
76B = Convertible/Interior Decor Group
65C = Hardtop Coupe/Bench Seat
76C = Convertible/Bench Seat

Color Codes
A = Raven Black
C = Honey Gold
D = Dynasty Green
F = Arcadian Blue (1966 color, used on late 1965s)
H = Caspian Blue
I = Champagne Beige
J = Rangoon Red
K = Silver Smoke Grey
M = Wimbledon White
O = Tropical Turquoise
P = Prairie Bronze
R = Ivy Green Metallic
X = Vintage Burgundy
Y = Silver Blue
Y = Skylight Blue

3 = Poppy Red
5 = Twilight Turquoise
7 = Phoenician Yellow
8 = Springtime Yellow

Trim Codes
Standard Interior
22 = Blue
25 = Red
26 = Black
27 = Aqua
29 = Palomino
D2 = Parchment
D3 = Parchment w/Burgundy Appointments
D5 = Parchment w/Red Appointments
D6 = Parchment w/Black Appointments
D7 = Parchment w/Aqua Appointments
D8 = Parchment w/Ivy Gold Appointments
D9 = Parchment w/Palomino Appointments

Interior Decor Group (also known as a Pony interior)
62 = Blue/White
65 = Red
66 = Black
67 = Aqua/White
68 = Ivy Gold/White
69 = Palomino
F2 = Parchment w/Blue Appointments
F3 = Parchment w/Burgundy Appointments
F4 = Parchment w/Emberglo Appointments
F5 = Parchment w/Red Appointments
F6 = Parchment w/Black Appointments
F7 = Parchment w/Aqua Appointments
F8 = Parchment w/Ivy Gold Appointments
F9 = Parchment w/Palomino Appointments

Bench Seat Interior
32 = Blue
35 = Red
36 = Black
39 = Palomino
C2 = Parchment w/Blue Appointments
C3 = Parchment w/Burgundy Appointments
C4 = Parchment w/Emberglo Appointments
C6 = Parchment w/Black Appointments
C7 = Parchment w/Aqua Appointments
C8 = Parchment w/Ivy Gold Appointments
C9 = Parchment w/Palomino Appointments

Date Codes
H = August 1964
J = September 1964
K = October 1964
L = November 1964

M = December 1964
A = January 1965
B = February 1965
Q = March 1965
R = April 1965
S = May 1965
T = June 1965
U = July 1965
V = August 1965
Note: The number (1–31) that appears before the month letter indicates the day.

DSO Codes (District Sales Office)
Note: 1965 DSOs were identical to 1964½.
11 = Boston
12 = Buffalo
13 = New York
14 = Pittsburgh
15 = Newark
21 = Atlanta
22 = Charlotte
23 = Philadelphia
24 = Jacksonville
25 = Richmond
26 = Washington, D.C.
31 = Cincinnati
32 = Cleveland
33 = Detroit
34 = Indianapolis
35 = Lansing
36 = Louisville
41 = Chicago
42 = Fargo
43 = Rockford
44 = Twin Cities
45 = Davenport
51 = Denver
52 = Des Moines
53 = Kansas City
54 = Omaha
55 = St. Louis
61 = Dallas
62 = Houston
63 = Memphis
64 = New Orleans
65 = Oklahoma City
71 = Los Angeles
72 = San Jose
73 = Salt Lake City
74 = Seattle
75 = Phoenix
81 = Ford of Canada
83 = U.S. Government
84 = Home Office Reserve
85 = American Red Cross
89 = Transportation Services
90–99 = Export

Axle Codes

CONVENTIONAL	LIMITED SLIP	AXLE RATIO
1	A	3.00:1
2	B	2.83:1
3	C	3.20:1
5	E	3.50:1
6	F	2.80:1
8	H	3.89:1
9	I	4.11:1

Transmission codes
1 = Three-Speed Manual
5 = Four-Speed Manual
6 = C-4 Dual-Range Cruise-O-Matic
F = C-4 Dual-Range Cruise-O-Matic (Canadian Export)

BODY SPECIFICATIONS

	Hardtop	Convertible	Fastback
Length (overall)	181.6"	181.6"	181.6"
Width (overall)	68.2"	68.2"	68.2"
Height (overall)	51.1"	51.0"	51.2"
Wheelbase	108.0"	108.0"	108.0"
Curb weight	2,610 lbs.	2,770 lbs.	2,640 lbs.
(Six-cyl., std. trans.)			

pertinent information relating to that particular Mustang.

Interior

Although similar to the earlier 1964½ interiors, a few changes marked the start of the 1965 model year production. Many of the minor changes are charted in chapter 2, which compares the small detail differences between the 1964½ and 1965 Mustangs. The biggest change for 1965 came in the form of a spectacular interior decor group, also know as the "pony interior." This option was made available in early spring, about the same time as the introduction of the GT package. Along with the interior decor group came a new instrument panel layout: the classic five-gauge cluster set against a simulated woodgrain backing. In addition to custom seat upholstery and door panels, the pony interior also featured woodgrain applique on the glove box door, console top plate, pistol-grip door handles, and steering wheel. The pony interior also meant new interior color choices and combinations. (All of the options are listed in the warranty plate decoding section.)

The five-gauge instrument cluster was also part of the GT equipment package. This version was set against an all-black "camera case" backing. Buyers who ordered a GT with a pony interior got the full woodgrain treatment. GT and pony interior speedometers registered up to 140 miles per hour.

Left: A very early 1965 seatbelt was a carryover from the old metal-against-metal style used on 1964½ Mustangs.

Below: The 1965 GT interior with full length console.

With the exception of an alternator light in place of a generator light, the base instrument panel layout on 1965 Mustangs was virtually identical to the 1964½.

Shortly after 1965 production began, all cars were equipped with an adjustable front passenger seat. The full bench seat became a regular production option on hardtops and convertibles, but of the nearly 1.3 million first-generation Mustangs produced, only about 2,000 were equipped with them. The transmission shifter was still floor mounted when the bench seat was specified.

The previously "white only" sun visors and headliners were now color-coded to the interior.

The new Mustang fastbacks featured all the appointments of the hardtop and convertible, plus a unique folding rear seat that quickly converted the rear passenger compartment into a stowage area with a flat load floor.

Out of all the first-generation Mustangs, 1965 models offered the most interior color choices. Up from a meager 12 in the 1964½s, the selection now offered 37 colors and color combination choices!

As a carryover feature from the early cars, convertible Mustangs featured a manually operated top that was designed with counterbalanced springs, providing easy operation of the relatively

Above: A full bench seat was offered in 1965. The bench seat came with a center folding armrest that when folded, at first glance, could be mistaken for a set of buckets! Below: The floor shifter (manual or automatic) remained in the same position as on bucket seat–equipped cars.

Left: The fastback's rear passenger compartment could be converted to a cavernous storage area in three easy steps. Below: Access to the trunk was permitted through a small steel door on fastback models.

Above: Outside air could be vented into the rear passenger compartment on fastback models through sliding controls located on the inner sail panels.

Above: On the GT instrument panel for 1965, note the change to the five-gauge cluster (from the standard "horizontal" version) and the presence of the optional Rally-Pac gauges. Rally-Pac gauges featured an 8,000-rpm tach on K-code cars, and a 6,000-rpm tach on all other Mustangs.

Remote-control mirror toggle switch was located at the lower portion of the driver's door.

GT models came equipped with a small ON-OFF switch that activated the dual fog lamps.

Above: Although the window crank and inner door handle changed slightly for 1965 (see full description in chapter 2), the door panel did not. The basic design was carried over from the earlier cars.

The day/night mirror was a dealer-installed option from 1964½ through the 1966 model year.

lightweight roof. An electrohydraulic power–operated top was optional.

Chassis

The platform-type chassis carried over through 1965 model year production on both hardtop and convertible Mustangs. The chassis remained unaltered with the introduction of the fastback 2+2 body style in September 1964.

As described in chapter 3, convertible Mustangs were equipped with torque boxes and additional all-steel reinforcements to provide proper chassis rigidity.

Regardless of engine size (six- or eight-cylinder), all Mustangs were based on the same platform chassis. An upgraded suspension compensated for the weight and power differences associated with the optional V-8 engines.

Engines

200-1V

By the time Ford was ready to start 1965 model year production, the humble 170-ci six-cylinder had changed a little. The big news was that Ford engineers bored it out once again, this time to a respectable 200 cubic inches, and redesigned it to include seven main bearings instead of the previous four. These, as well as several other major revisions, resulted in a vastly improved little powerplant. The new engine was best described by Ford: "Redesigned for 1965, the 200-ci Six is now standard in the Mustang, Fairlane, and four-door Falcon Futura and Squire Station Wagons. It is optional in all other Falcons and the Falcon Station Bus and Club Wagons. Horsepower has been increased to 120 without a corresponding increase in gas consumption. Larger valves and changes in valve cooling, combined with camshaft modifications have allowed Ford engineers to 'squeeze' additional performance from an already efficient engine. Compression on the '200' Six has been raised from 8.7 to 9.2:1 and with the new valving arrangement, regular gas is still used for most efficient operation.

"Seven main bearings now make a smoother running, longer lasting engine, adding increased owner satisfaction again in 1965. For improved lubrication, a new larger oil pump has been installed to handle the higher horsepower and larger bearing surfaces. As on Ford's other six-cylinder engines, the '200' Six features an automatic choke this year. Economy is further increased by this dual-control choke which senses not only the temperature of the exhaust manifold, but also the engine coolant temperature for improved starts when the engine is semi-warm."

Visually, the new 200 looked almost identical to the 170 from 1964½: an all-black engine block, cylinder head, and intake manifold were finished with a bright red valve cover and air cleaner.

The 1965 also marked the start of the alternator charging system on all Ford engines.

(For a complete description of the color schemes associated with 1965 engines, please see chapter 1.)

Exhaust

Basically identical to the 1964½ 170 exhaust system, the 200 featured a single muffler mounted parallel to, and directly behind, the rear axle. The muffler was 25 inches long, offering a less-restrictive airflow and more optimal tuning.

289-2V

One of the big changes for all 1965 289s was in the bellhousing bolt configuration. The entire bellhousing area was enlarged to fit over an 11-inch clutch on certain 289 applications. However, regardless of the clutch size used, the bellhousing was now attached to the block using six bolts instead of five. In a nutshell, the difference in the number of bolts used led to the phrase "five-bolt" when referring to pre-1965 289s, and "six-bolt" as the ID for 1965 and later engines.

With the move to the alternator charging system for 1965, revisions had to be made elsewhere in the engine compartment: New lightweight mounting brackets were used with a large $\frac{7}{16}$-inch bolt to secure the alternator. Along with it came changes to the mounting bolt holes in the cylinder head. The position of the oil dipstick tube was also affected by the presence of the lower-mounted alternator, because it had to be moved closer to the cylinder head and shortened by 5 inches. (Numerous smaller revisions ensued with the charging system change, and space does not

permit us to list them all here. Many of the details are listed in Bob Mannel's excellent guidebook, *Mustang & Ford Small Block V-8, Vols. 1 & 2*, by RPM Press).

With the 260-ci V-8 now discontinued by Ford, the 289-2V small block was slated as the standard V-8 engine offering in 1965 Mustangs. Rated at an even 200 horsepower, the 289-2V's piston and combustion chamber configuration was essentially the same as 1964's 289-2V, the engine used to power full-size Galaxies and LTDs. Needless to say, Ford was fairly confident in offering it as a baseline V-8 for the much lighter Mustang.

Sometimes referred to as the "Challenger V-8," Ford's ad copy raved about this engine in 1965: "The most popular by far of all Ford engines, the 289-2V engine combines performance, economy and low maintenance to make it one of the best engines that has ever been designed by Ford engineers. Lightweight, powerful, and quiet, it provides almost ideal power for all vehicles, from the smallest Falcon to the largest Ford. Hydraulic valve lifters, pedestal-mounted rocker arms and large valves provide quiet, efficient operation with a minimum of maintenance. The two-venturi carburetor provides economy of operation combined with efficient fuel distribution to provide smooth operation. The dual-advance distributor is calibrated to provide full spark control over a wide range of engine speeds and load conditions. Autolite power-tip sparkplugs are self-cleaning, and perform efficiently over their entire life range."

The 289-2V received a minor piston change midway through 1965 production. As they became available, new pistons with valve reliefs replaced the earlier dish-shaped units without valve reliefs. The new pistons were less "dished" to compensate for the new valve relief volume, so the engine's compression ratio was unaffected.

BASE EQUIPMENT ENGINE: T-CODE	
Type:	Six cylinder, inline, overhead valve
Displacement:	200 cubic inches
Foundry group:	Fairlane "Six"
Bore and stroke:	3.68x3.13
Maximum compression ratio: (with standard gaskets)	9.2:1
Gross horsepower at 4,400 rpm:	120
Gross torque at 2,400 rpm:	190 ft.-lbs.
Valve lifters:	Hydraulic
Carburetor:	Autolite 1100, 1V
Recommended fuel:	Regular
Emission controls CA only:	N/A
Emission controls 49 states:	N/A
Dimensions:	33"L x 33"W x 28"H
Weight:	360 lbs.

OPTIONAL EQUIPMENT ENGINE: C-CODE	
Type:	Eight-cylinder, 90-degree V, overhead valve
Displacement:	289 cubic inches
Foundry group:	Fairlane V8
Bore and stroke:	4.00x2.87
Maximum compression ratio: (with standard gaskets)	9.3:1
Gross horsepower at 4,400 rpm:	200
Gross torque at 2,400 rpm:	282 ft.-lbs.
Valve lifters:	Hydraulic
Carburetor:	Autolite 2100, 2V
Recommended fuel:	Regular
Emission controls CA only:	N/A
Emission controls 49 states:	N/A
Dimensions:	28"L x 25"W x 29"H
Weight:	460 lbs.

The 289-2V C-code sported the typical 1965 color scheme: black block with gold valve covers and air cleaner. The photo on the right shows a car with optional air conditioning.

Exhaust

The 289-2V's exhaust system is virtually identical to the 289-4V setup offered in 1964½ Mustangs. Dual pipes run from the exhaust manifolds then merge and connect in a V near where the transmission joins the driveshaft. The full-length single pipe runs the length of the chassis, then loops up and over the rear axle and connects to a single, transversely mounted muffler. The muffler is positioned between the rear axle and the gas tank.

289-4V

The 1965 version of the 289-4V featured a higher compression ratio than its 1964 counterpart. The new 10.0:1 compression ratio (versus 1964's 9.4:1) was due to the implementation of flat-top pistons, similar in design to the lethal K-code's. Increased compression dictated the need for premium grade fuel, leading Ford to refer to the engine as the "premium-fueled 289-4V."

Sales literature in 1965 spoke to those who didn't mind paying a little extra at the pumps: "For those who require more power in the Mustang, this engine provides a healthy 225 brake horsepower. Specially designed to utilize the extra power in premium fuel, the '289' Premium Fuel engine has several refinements over the standard '289.' Revised valve timing and a higher compression ratio, piston design similar to that of the Hi-Performance '289' V-8, and a unique ignition system allow this engine to fully utilize the premium fuel required for optimum performance. The recalibrated four-venturi carburetor and a low-restriction air cleaner allow maximum efficiency and most economical fuel-air mixtures. Alternate spacing of intake and exhaust valves assures higher volumetric efficiency and elimination of 'hot spots' in the cylinder heads."

Midway through the 1965 production year, as they became available, the 289-4V received new pistons with valve reliefs. The valve reliefs increased the chamber volume just enough to lower the compression ratio slightly to 9.8:1.

The change to the alternator charging system (with the associated mounting bracket and oil dipstick revisions) also affected the 289-4V.

Exhaust

With the 289-4V engine, the standard exhaust system mimicked the 289-2Vs. On early 1965 cars

The A-code 289 was similar in appearance to the two-barrel C-code engine. This one pumped out an additional 25 horses and enjoyed a healthy 10.0:1 compression ratio. The electronic ignition wiring pictured was not stock.

OPTIONAL EQUIPMENT ENGINE: A-CODE

Type:	Eight-cylinder, 90-degree V, overhead valve
Displacement:	289 cubic inches
Foundry group:	Fairlane V8
Bore and stroke:	4.00x2.87
Maximum compression ratio: (with standard gaskets)	10.0:1
Gross horsepower at 4,800 rpm:	225
Gross torque at 3,200 rpm:	305 ft.-lbs.
Valve lifters:	Hydraulic
Carburetor:	Autolite 4100, 4V
Recommended fuel:	Premium
Emission controls CA only:	N/A
Emission controls 49 states:	N/A
Dimensions:	28"L x 25"W x 29"H
Weight:	465 lbs.

OPTIONAL EQUIPMENT ENGINE: K-CODE

Type:	Eight-cylinder, 90-degree V, overhead valve
Displacement:	289 cubic inches
Foundry group:	Fairlane V8
Bore and stroke:	4.00x2.87
Maximum compression ratio: (with standard gaskets)	10.5:1
Gross horsepower at 6,000 rpm:	271
Gross torque at 3,400 rpm:	312 ft.-lbs.
Valve lifters:	Solid/adjustable
Carburetor:	Autolite 4100, 4V
Recommended fuel:	Super Premium
Emission controls CA only:	N/A
Emission controls 49 states:	N/A
Dimensions:	28"L x 25"W x 29"H
Weight:	465 lbs.

The magnificent 289-4V "hi-po" small block. Like all the other engines for 1965, the K-code received a black block. Chrome valve covers and a chrome air cleaner completed the custom high-performance look.

(after mid-August 1964), the optional dual exhaust system was identical to the 1964½ K-code 289 hi-po system. After October 15, 1965, the dual exhaust system changed to a free-flow setup. The engine's individual exhaust manifolds were connected to dual exhaust pipes that ran back along the length of the chassis where they fit into two separate mufflers that were located in front of the rear axle. The pipes then exited the mufflers, looped up and over the axle, and ran through a set of smaller resonators. Then the twin tailpipes exited beneath the rear valance. On A-codes with the GT option (after late February 1965), the twin tailpipes exited through special holes in the rear valance panel.

289-4V "Hi Po"
Like all 289s, the Hi-Performance version went to the six-bolt bellhousing configuration. Other than this and the change to the alternator charging system (with the associated mounting bracket and oil dipstick revisions), the K-code 289 remained unchanged from its 1964½ predecessor. What did change significantly however, was the exhaust system design.

Exhaust
The 289 hi-po exhaust system was now classified as a free-flow setup. Individual header-type exhaust manifolds were connected to an H-pipe located near the base of the transmission housing.

Then, dual exhaust pipes ran back along the length of the chassis where they fit into two separate mufflers that are located in front of the rear axle. The pipes exited the mufflers, looped up and over the axle, and ran through a set of smaller resonators. The system ended with twin tailpipes exiting beneath the rear valance. On K-codes with the GT option (after late February 1965), the twin tailpipes exited through special holes in the rear valance panel.

Transmissions

All transmissions carried over from early 1964½ production through the 1965 model year. Some changes in applications and gear ratios were made, however. As before, six-cylinder Mustangs received the conventional three-speed nonsynchro transmissions as base equipment.

With the exception of the K-coded engines, all V-8–powered Mustangs came standard with the constant mesh fully synchronized three-speed transmission as standard equipment. The 260-2V V-8 engine was no longer available in the Mustang line.

Above: The Autolite 4100 series four-barrel carburetor featured an automatic choke and a rating of 480 cubic feet per minute.

K-codes also received special high-strength motor mounts specifically designed to endure higher rpms.

Opposite: Comparison photos of the K-code (top) and A-code (bottom) valve train indicate the major differences. The hi-po cylinder heads (top) are definitely stronger than the garden-variety 289 heads, and they feature deeper cast-in spring seats. Note the adjustable rocker arm studs. (The nuts underneath the rocker arms are not present on the A-code's valve train.) The rocker arm studs on K-codes were threaded in, not pressed, which helped them resist pulling out at high rpm. The valve springs were different, too. Hi-po springs had a higher compression rating of 350 pounds per inch, while "standard" 289 springs were rated at 250 pounds per inch. Smaller "damper" springs were also fitted inside the larger springs on Ks. They helped close the valve faster at high rpms.

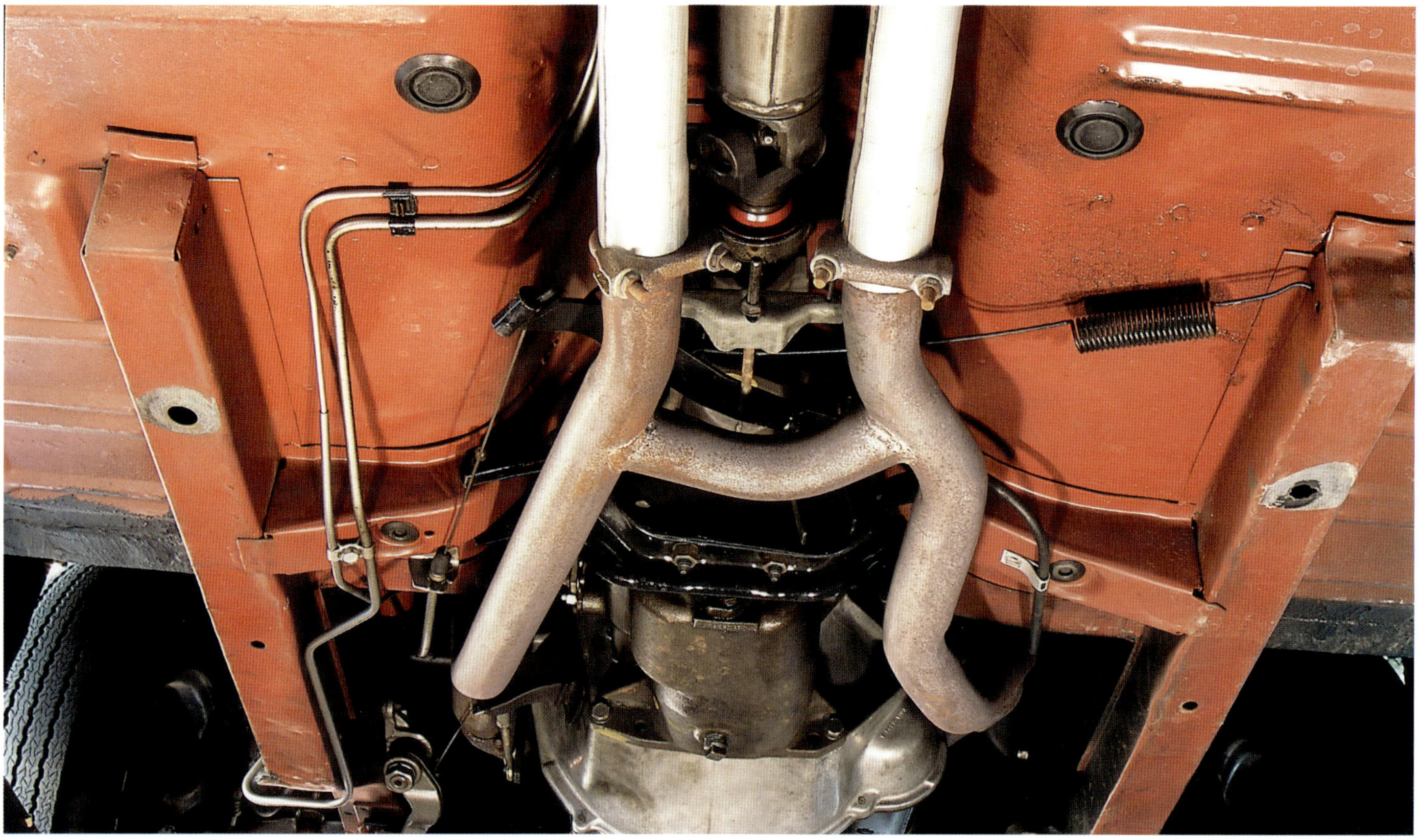

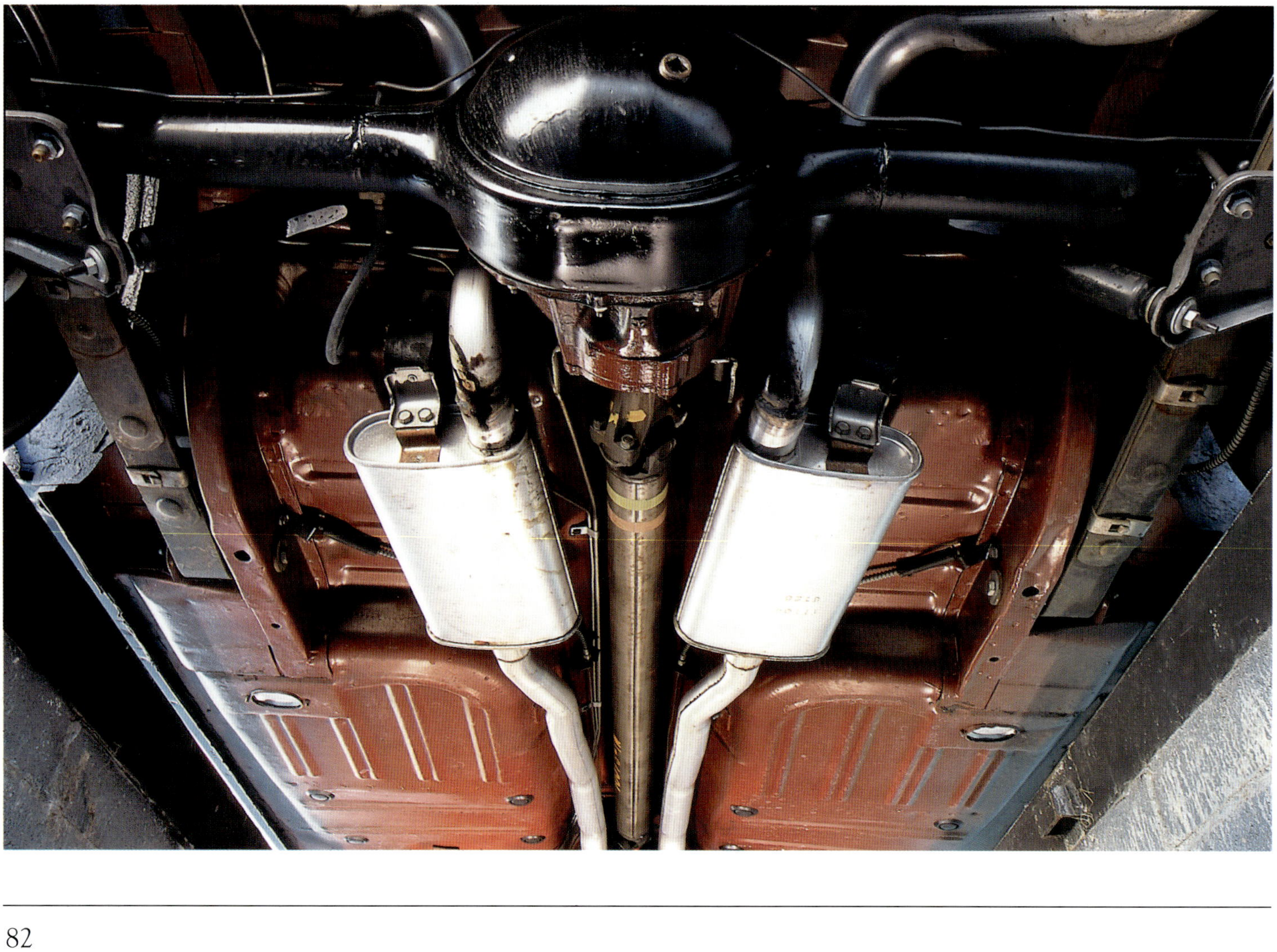

Clutches

Clutch design and configuration remained unchanged throughout the 1965 model year. Six-cylinder cars utilized noncentrifugal clutches, while eight-cylinder Mustangs used semicentrifugal units.

All clutches on manual transmission Mustangs were of a single-disc, dry plate configuration.

Rear Axles

Six-Cylinder Models

Identical to the early 1964½ system, Mustangs equipped with six-cylinder engines came with a rear axle housing made of cast-iron. The deep offset drive pinion was supported by two tapered roller bearings positioned just ahead of the ring gear. The axle shafts were made from induction-hardened steel forgings with cold-rolled splines at the ends that connected to the differential, and wheel hub flanges at the outer ends.

Eight-Cylinder Models

A carryover from the early cars, V-8 Mustangs featured a rear axle with a straddle-mounted pinion and a banjo-type housing. This design gave bearing support on both sides of the pinion, keeping the pinion and ring gear in constant alignment. Eight-cylinder differentials featured two tapered roller bearings located ahead of the pinion gear and a straight roller bearing located

CONVENTIONAL SIX-CYLINDER THREE-SPEED MANUAL GEAR RATIOS	
First	2.76:1
Second	1.69:1
Third	1.00:1
Reverse	3.74:1

CONVENTIONAL V8 CONSTANT MESH THREE-SPEED MANUAL GEAR RATIOS	
First	2.79:1
Second	1.70:1
Third	1.00:1
Reverse	2.87:1

FOUR-SPEED MANUAL TRANSMISSION GEAR RATIOS (SIX-CYLINDER)	
First	3.16:1
Second	2.21:1
Third	1.41:1
Fourth	1.00:1
Reverse	3.34:1

FOUR-SPEED MANUAL TRANSMISSION GEAR RATIOS (289-2V, 4V AND 289-4V HI-PERFORMANCE)		
	289-2V, 4V	289-4V "hi-po"
First	2.78:1	2.32:1
Second	1.93:1	1.69:1
Third	1.36:1	1.29:1
Fourth	1.00:1	1.00:1
Reverse	2.78:1	2.32:1

CRUISE-O-MATIC GEAR RATIOS (ALL ENGINES EXCEPT 289-4V HI-PERFORMANCE		
First		2.46:1
Second		1.46:1
Third		1.00:1
Reverse		2.20:1
Converter Ratio:	Six-cyl.	2.40:1
	Eight-cyl.	2.05:1

behind the gear. This design provided proper support for the pinion shaft, both fore and aft. The individual axles were made from induction-hardened steel forgings with cold-rolled splines that connected with the differential, and wheel hub flanges at the outer ends.

Driveshaft and Universal Joints

Every Mustang was assembled with an exposed driveshaft attached by universal joints at either end. The driveshafts were manufactured using seamless steel tubing that offered maximum strength and lightweight construction. Forged yokes were welded at both ends, then the entire unit was precision balanced.

Universal joints were the cross-and-yoke type, featuring sealed, prelubricated needle bearings. Service was required at 36,000-mile intervals.

Suspension, Steering, Brakes

Suspension systems on 1965 model year Mustangs were identical to the earlier 1964½ cars. The heavy-duty suspension system came as standard equipment with the 289 Hi-Performance V-8 and on cars equipped with the GT package. It was optional on all other Mustangs equipped with a V-8 engine.

Steering

The steering systems (both manual and power) from the early 1964½ Mustangs carried over throughout the 1965 model year. All cars were equipped with a parallelogram linkage–type steering system that used a cross-link and idler arm setup. The steering gear was a recirculating ball-and-nut type, identified by the trademark "Magic Circle." All friction points within the entire steering linkage were permanently lubricated. The steering box (and gear) was filled with a life-of-car lubricant.

The optional power steering system is proportional in design. Maximum steering effort required to activate the full power assist is 4 pounds of pressure. An Eaton-type power steering pump and reservoir were located near the front of the engine compartment, off to the left side of the motor. As demand increased, Ford continued to use pumps manufactured by Eaton as well as their own FoMoCo brand.

The special handling package and the power steering option (by itself) both offered the quicker gear ratio (22:1).

Brakes

The braking system for both six- and eight-cylinder Mustangs remained unchanged from the early cars. The drum-type brakes were single-anchor, self-energizing, internal expanding, and air-cooled. Self-adjusters would automatically adjust the brake linings as required when the brakes were applied while the car was moving in reverse. The self-adjusters would also help maintain the proper brake pedal height.

The hydraulics of the Mustang's braking system utilized a jar-type cap and a diaphragm-type gasket that sealed the system against the outside elements.

The parking/emergency brake was conventional in design, and was engaged by a twist-and-release handle located under the left side of the instrument panel.

The optional front disc brakes could be ordered on 1965 Mustangs equipped with a V-8 engine. The brakes incorporated a cast-iron disc

AXLE BUILD TAGS

Both six-cylinder and V-8 Mustangs carried an ID tag on the differential at the point of assembly. In chapter 1, we briefly covered how to decode the information on an axle build tag. The following table identifies the differential type and the particular unit's application.

Tag#	Diameter	Ratio	Type	Application Notes
WCY-E	7.25"	3.20	Conventional, 2 pin	
WCY-F	7.25"	3.50	Conventional, 2 pin	With manual transmission only
WCY-L	7.25"	3.20	Equa lock, 2 pin	
WCY-N	7.25"	2.83	Conventional, 2 pin	With manual transmission only
WCY-R	7.25"	2.83	Conventional, 2 pin	With automatic transmission only
WCY-AA	7.25"	2.83	Equa lock, 2 pin	
WCY-AJ	7.25"	3.20	Conventional, 2 pin	
WCZ-E	8.00"	2.80	Conventional, 2 pin	With 289-2V
WCZ-F	8.00"	3.00	Conventional, 2 pin	With 289-4V and three-speed manual or auto
WCZ-G	8.00"	3.50	Conventional, 2 pin	With 289-4V and four-speed
WCZ-H	8.75"	3.89	Conventional, 2 pin	With 289 K and four-speed
WCZ-J	8.75"	4.11	Conventional, 2 pin	With 289 K and four-speed
WCZ-P	8.75"	3.50	Conventional, 2 pin	High-performance applications only
WDJ-B	7.75"	2.80	Equa lock, 2 pin	
WDJ-C	8.00"	3.00	Equa lock, 2 pin	289-4V with all transmission types
WDJ-E	8.00"	3.50	Equa lock, 2 pin	289 K and four-speed

with a brake pad on either side. Each brake pad was actuated by two brake cylinders. The disc was a one-piece casting with radial ribs separating the two sides of the disc, allowing air circulation for maximum heat dissipation. Rear brakes were of the standard drum design.

A rear axle ID tag was affixed to the differential housing on all Mustangs. (Deciphering an axle tag was discussed in chapter 1.)

Top left and right: The heavy-duty suspension on this Mustang is correctly restored with the proper silver paint (simulating bare metal) on the upper control arms(A). Note the red paint daubs on the stiffer high-performance spring. Above left: Silver paint was also used on the lower control arm (simulating bare metal). All Mustang suspensions were similar in design; the V-8s were beefed up to compensate for added weight and performance. Above right: A daub of paint was applied to the tie rod/steering knuckle connection to further identify the assembly's configuration.

STEERING SPECIFICATIONS

Linkage:	Parallelogram with cross-link and idler arm
Gear type:	"Magic Circle" recirculating ball
Overall steering ratio:	
Manual	27:1
Power	22:1
Turns (lock to lock):	
Manual	4.5
Power	3.7
Turning diameter:	38.9 feet

Steering gear box build tags	
1965	**Tag ID**
Manual steering (standard):	HCC-AT
Manual steering (performance):	HCC-AX
Power steering:	HCC-AW

Power-assisted brakes were optional, but could not be ordered in combination with disc brakes. The vacuum-operated power booster was manufactured by Bendix on all 1965 model cars and featured an adjustable pushrod with tolerances between .980 inch and .995 inch.

Electrical, Cooling, Heating

Although the exact date is not known, sometime near the start of 1965 production, the switch was made to an alternator-based charging system. In conjunction with a 12-volt electrical system, base Mustangs utilized a 38-ampere alternator and a simplified regulator. A-code, K-code, and cars equipped with air conditioning received 42-amp units. The new alternators featured sealed bearings and built-in shields that protected them from road dirt and moisture. Ford's reasoning served to educate the buyer: "The alternator system has the advantage of more positive battery charging, especially at low engine speeds in stop-and-go city driving. In addition, the charging rate of the alternator system is higher than the previous direct-current generator, a feature that helps reduce the possibility of battery failure when using air conditioners or other high electrical usage options."

Standard equipment batteries also changed with the introduction of the alternator. According to early 1965 Ford literature, ". . . the new batteries feature inner cell connections for greater

Right top: Optional disc brakes included a four-piston caliper set-up with 11-inch rotors. When this option was specified, power assist was not available.
Right middle: This shot shows the disc brake's proportioning valve.

BRAKE SPECIFICATIONS

	Six-Cylinder	Eight-Cylinder
Brake drum diameter:	9 in.	10 in.
Lining material:	Molded asbestos	
Lining attachment:	Riveted	
Total lining area (sq. in.):	131.0	154.2

corrosion resistance and higher strength . . . additional electrolyte capacity for less frequent need to add water, and an increased plate area for improved cold starting characteristics." A heavy-duty battery was available as either a factory- or dealer-installed option.

The early radiators were carried over into the 1965 model year. Six-cylinder cars used an 8½-quart capacity unit; V-8–powered cars received 14-quart versions. Both radiators were fully pressurized and regulated by thermostats located at the upper engine outlet on both six- and eight-cylinder cars.

Non-air-conditioned Mustangs used four-bladed fans, while a/c-equipped cars used a five-bladed fan mounted to a stamped-steel engine pulley.

Optional air conditioning units were produced by Ford and were mounted directly under the center of the instrument panel. On 1965 cars, the face of the air conditioner was painted dull silver and featured four circular bezels to direct airflow. The fan featured three speeds: High (6.5–7.5 amps), Medium (4.5–5.5 amps), and Low (3–4 amps). All air-conditioner compressors were located near the front of the engine and were typically belt-driven units. Air conditioning circuit protection was provided by a 3AG 15-amp fuse.

Mustang heaters were located underneath the passenger side of the instrument panel and used water heated and circulated from the engine to operate. Revised blower motors could be now be operated at three different fan speeds: High (6–8 amps), Medium (4–6 amps), and Low (2–4 amps). The heater/blower used a circuit protector with a SFE 14-amp fuse.

Right: A 38-ampere Autolite alternator replaced the old FoMoCo generators from early 1964. Mustangs equipped with K-code or A-code engines received 42-amp alternators, as did air-conditioned cars.

Left top: A properly date-coded and tagged distributor and corresponding sparkplug wires are shown on a 1965 K-code 289 Hi-Performance V-8. Left middle: A close-up overhead view shows the wire routing for the GT's fog lamps. Correct routing was through small holes drilled in the radiator core support. Left bottom: Cooling system protection labels were applied to all radiator tops. The radiator cap shown is a reproduction, not an original. Below: The air conditioner's control center was located underneath the center of the instrument panel. Identical to their earlier counterparts, 1965 air conditioners received a matte silver finish control panel.

Wheels and Tires

Continued from 1964 and used throughout the 1965 model year, both six- and eight-cylinder Mustangs came standard with 13-inch wheels. K-coded cars were the exception with 14-inch wheels. The wheels for the six-cylinder had a four-lug pattern, while the wheels for the V-8 were five-lug. Both styles had a bead width of 4½ inches. Fourteen-inch wheels were optional on both six- and eight-cylinder Mustangs. The special handling package (which included 14-inch wheels and tires, as well as a heavy-duty suspension) was optional on all V-8–powered cars, and of course, was standard equipment on 289-4V K-code Mustangs. After September 1964, the 15-inch wheel option was dropped.

Nineteen sixty-five Mustangs (both six- and eight-cylinder versions) came standard with 6.50"x13" four-ply rayon black sidewall tires.

High-grade nylon tires and white sidewall versions were optional on both the 13-inch and 14-inch sizes. The 15-inch tires were dropped in September 1964 in favor of the dual red line 14-inch nylon tires. The dual red line rubber was offered as standard equipment on the K-code cars, and was optional on all other Mustangs equipped with V-8 engines.

Carried over as a feature from the early cars, eight-cylinder Mustangs with air conditioning received the 6.95"x13" tires as standard equipment.

In the fall of 1964, all tires went to a lower-profile format, and the 6.50"x14" tires were discontinued in favor of the heavier 6.95"x14" size.

All 13-inch and 14-inch tires were available with white sidewalls.

WHEEL SPECIFICATIONS

Type:	Six-Cylinder	Eight-Cylinder
	Stamped-steel ventilated disc with safety-type rims	
Number of studs:	4	5
Diameter and rim size:		
Standard	13"x4.5"	13"x4.5"
Optional	14"x4.5"	14"x5"

TIRE SPECIFICATIONS

	6.50" x13"	6.95" x13"	6.95" x14"	5.60"/ 5.90"x15"
Six-cyl.	std.	-	opt.	-
Eight-cyl.	-	std.	opt.	opt.
Eight-cyl.*	-	-	std.	opt.

*with handling package

Above: Optional wheel cover for 13-inch or 14-inch applications featured a knock-off–style center cap. Below left: The standard wheel cover for all Mustangs came in 13-inch and 14-inch versions. Below: Optional deluxe wheel cover for 13-inch or 14-inch applications.

Right: Optional wire wheel cover for 14-inch applications was introduced in the fall of 1964. Far right: Optional styled steel wheels were available in 14-inch, five-lug pattern applications only. The wheel was scheduled as a regular production option in the early summer of 1964.

OPTIONS

The following list of options appeared in 1965 model dealer pricing literature. The biggest changes over 1964½ were the addition of the GT Performance Package, a deluxe interior decor group, and the choice of three V-8 engines—all based on the 289-ci motor. A sharp eye will note that most of the suggested retail prices were actually lower in 1965. This reduction resulted because a lot of Ford's newly developed tooling had already paid for itself. Chalk it up to rabid sales.

Base Price:
2-Door Hardtop:	$2,320.96
Convertible:	$2,557.64
2+2 Fastback:	$2,533.19

Engines:
•8-Cylinder 289-CID 2V 200-HP	$105.63
(extra charge over 200-CID 1V 120-HP six-cylinder)	
•8-Cylinder 289-CID 4V 225-HP	$52.85
(extra charge over 289-CID 2V)	
•8-Cylinder 289-CID 4V 271-HP Hi-Performance	$327.92
(extra charge over 289-CID 2V, includes Special Handling Package and 6.95x14 Dual Red Band Nylon Tires) N/A with GT Equip Group	
•With GT Equipment Group	$276.34

Transmissions:
•Cruise-O-Matic Six-Cylinder	$175.80
•Cruise-O-Matic 200/225-HP V-8	$185.39
•Four-Speed Manual Six-Cylinder	$113.45
•Four-Speed Manual V-8	$184.02

Performance Equipment:
•Disc Brakes, Front, 8-Cyl. (N/A with power brakes)	$56.77
•Limited Slip Differential	$41.60
•Rally Pac w/Clock/Tachometer	$69.30
•Special Handling Package for 200- and 225-HP V-8 Engines	$30.64
(includes increased-rate front and rear springs, larger front and rear shock absorbers, 22:1 steering ratio, and larger-diameter front stabilizer bar)	
•GT Equipment Group	$165.03
(available with 225- and 271-HP V-8 engines only: includes dual exhaust system with bright extensions through valance panel, Special Handling Package components, front disc brakes, fog lamps and grille bar, GT stripe, five-dial instrument cluster, and GT ornamentation)	
•Wheels, Styled Steel, 14-inch (V-8 only)	$119.71

Power Assists:
•Power Brakes	$42.29
•Power Steering	$107.08
(includes unique luxury trim, padded visors, woodgrain applique ornamentation, and R/W door courtesy lights)	
•Full-Width Seat with Center Armrest (hardtop and convertible)	$24.42
•Glass, Tinted with Banded Windshield	$30.25
•Windshield Only, Tinted and Banded	$21.09
•Radio, Push Button and Antenna	$57.51
•Rocker Panel Molding (hardtop and convertible)	$15.76

•Steering Wheel, Deluxe	$31.52
•Vinyl Roof (hardtop)	$74.19
•Wheel Covers w/Knock-Off Hubs	$17.82
•Wire Wheel Covers, 14-inch	$44.83
•Magic Aire Heater, Delete (Credit)	($31.52)
•Seat Belts, Delete (Credit)	($10.76)

Optional Tire Prices:
Five 6.50x13 BSW Rayon tires as standard equipment on all six-cylinder models.
Extra charge for:
•6.50x13 WSW	$33.30
•6.95x14 BSW	$7.36
•6.95x14 WSW	$40.67

Five 6.95x14 BSW tires as standard equipment on all eight-cylinder models, except the 271-HP Hi-Performance engine.
Extra charge for:
•6.95x14 WSW	$33.31
•6.95x14 BSW Nylon	$15.67
•6.95x14 WSW Nylon	$48.89
•6.95x14 Dual Red Band, Nylon	$48.97

Dealer-Installed Accessories:
•Door Edge Guards	$2.70
•Rocker Panel Molding (set)	$19.10
•Wheel Covers, Deluxe with Spinner (13 in.)	$28.95
•Wheel Covers, Deluxe with Spinner (14 in.)	$28.95
•Wheel Covers, Simulated Wire (13 in.)	$58.35
•Wheel Covers, Simulated Wire (14 in.)	$58.35
•Luggage Rack	$35.00
•Tonneau Cover (White)	$52.70
•Tonneau Cover (Black)	$52.70
•L.H. Spot Light	$29.95
•Vanity Mirror	$1.95
•License Plate Frame	$4.50
•Fire Extinguisher	$33.70
•Compass	$7.95
•AM Radio	$53.50
•Rear Seat Speaker	$11.95
•Studio Sonic Sound System (Reverb)	$22.95
•Round (Cone-Shaped) Outside Mirror	$3.95
•Left-Hand Remote Mirror	$2.25
•Universal (Flat) Outside Mirror	$12.75
•Matching Right Hand	$6.95
•Inside Day-Night Mirror	$4.95
•Back-Up Lights	$10.40
•Power Brakes	$47.00
•Glove Box Lock	$2.49
•Remote Control Trunk Release	$6.95
•Windshield Washers	$14.50
•Rally-Pac (Six-cylinder)	$75.95
•Rally-Pac (Eight-cylinder)	$75.95

Chapter 5

1966

Nineteen sixty-six was (and as of this writing still is) Mustang's most successful year ever. August 1965 marked the start of 1966 model production, and even then, after nearly a year and a half on the market, Mustangs were still the hottest cars in America. By now Ford had coined the term ponycar, and had created a full-blown legend. And with three assembly plants working around the clock, a buyer could now walk into any dealership in the country and drive away in the Mustang of his or her choice. M-cars had literally saturated the marketplace, and no end was in sight. People were still buying Mustangs as fast as Ford could build them.

At first glance, 1966 Mustangs looked identical to their 1965 predecessors. Why mess with success? Styling refinements were the order of the day. Most Mustang owners will quickly point out the most obvious change: the revised grille. In addition to a myriad of trim revisions, several safety upgrades included the addition of reverse lights as a standard feature, rear seat belts, and

Opposite, above, and right: This 1966 Mustang GT convertible, 289 four-barrel, came equipped in "new for '66" Nightmist Blue (paint code K). The most obvious change for the 1966 cars was the revised grille.

1966 EQUIPMENT

- Air Cleaner Filter: 36,000 miles
- Accelerator Pedal: Suspended Type
- Alternator: 38 amps
- Ash Tray: Front
- Armrests: Front
- Armrests and Ash Trays: Rear (convertible)
- Back-Up Lights
- Battery: "Sta-Ful" Design
- Body: Rust Resistant
- Brakes: Self-Adjusting
- Bucket Seats: Foam Padded, Adjustable
- Carpets: Nylon, Rayon Molded
- Choke: Automatic
- Cigarette Lighter
- Coat Hooks
- Coolant: 2-years or 36,000 miles
- Courtesy Lights, Front: Door Switches
- Courtesy Lights, Rear: Door Switches (fastback)
- Curved Side Glass
- Door Checks: 2-Stage
- Door Hinges: Bronze Bushed
- Door Latches: Safety Type
- Door Trim: All Vinyl
- Emergency Flashers
- Engine: 200-ci six-cylinder
- Finish: Super Diamond Lustre Enamel
- Front Fenders: Bolt-On
- Fuel Filter: 36,000 miles
- Fuel Tank: 16 gallons
- Glass: Safety
- Glove Box Light
- Headlining: Color Keyed Vinyl (except convertible)
- Heater and Defroster: Fresh Air

- Hood Latch: Single Action
- Horns: Dual
- Instrument Panel: Padded
- Insulated Body
- Jack: Scissors Type, Body Side
- Lamp Bulbs: Extended Life
- Lubrication, Chassis: 36,000 miles
- Maintenance: Twice a Year
- Mirror: Inside Rearview
- Mirror: Outside Rearview
- Molding: Rocker Panel
- Muffler: Aluminized
- Oil Filter: 6,000 miles
- Scuff Plates: Aluminum
- Seat Belts: Front and Rear
- Rear Seat: Folding (fastback)
- Steering Wheel: Deep Dish, Safety Type
- Sun Visors: Padded, Color-Keyed
- Thermostat: 195 Degrees
- Transmission Lever: Tunnel mounted
- Transmission: Three-Speed Manual
- Turn Signals
- Upholstery: All Vinyl
- Upholstery: Cloth and Vinyl (except convertible)
- Valve Lifters: Hydraulic
- Ventilation: Cowl Aire intakes (except fastback)
- Ventilation: Cowl Aire plus Roof Vent Outlets (fastback)
- Wheel Covers: Full
- Windshield Washers
- Windshield Wipers: 15-inch Electric

About as basic as it gets (and still absolutely gorgeous), this 1966 convertible is a six-cylinder, three-speed manual car with very little in the way of optional equipment. Paint is Candyapple red Apple Red (paint code T).

A rare 1966 K-code convertible GT in Ivy Green Metallic (paint code R), this car is an "as is" survivor. It is unrestored but still in incredible condition!

emergency flashers. Although not drastically changed from 1965, Ford boasted Mustang's new list of standard equipment for 1966.

On March 2, 1966, the "Millionth Mustang" rolled off the line at Dearborn. This milestone, of course, provided a perfect excuse for Ford to throw a party. According to folklore and various magazine features of the day, every Ford district sales office received a millionth anniversary Mustang. The cars were all hardtop coupes (still the biggest seller by far) painted a special Anniversary Gold. Apparently, no paint code was listed on the warranty plate, and each car received a unique six-digit DSO code.

The big anniversary party also marked the introduction of the Mustang Sprint 200. It was springtime, and Ford's clever marketing strategy invited everyone to "Join our Millionth Mustang Success Sale!" Sprint 200s were, as the name implies, six-cylinder Mustangs with a dress-up package aimed at further increasing sales. In actuality, Ford wanted to encourage the sale of more six-cylinder cars, because V-8 engine production couldn't keep up with demand. The full-page ad went on to identify all the benefits of "Limited Production" Sprint 200 ownership.

A super-sweet 1966 hardtop GT in Emberglo (paint code V) sparkles in the mid-afternoon sun.

Newspaper and magazine ads in 1966 were somewhat tame when compared to the madcap spots used in 1965. "Mustang! Mustang! Mustang!" was the catchphrase used as the sign-off on print ads as well as sales brochures. Reflecting the subtle refinements of the new models, one ad read: "If you thought we couldn't improve on a winner—try Mustang '66!" After the catchy headline, the ad copy was written in a soothing manner, comforting people that their favorite car hadn't changed much, and now it offered more creature comforts, more options, and a better selection of colors. The ads didn't mislead, either. The new Mustangs were more refined, and prices were still an absolute bargain. Base price for the hardtop was now $2,416, up only $95 from last year. The convertible saw the same increase, stickered at $2,652. Fastback base prices went up by $73, now at $2,607.

Nineteen sixty-six had been a banner year for Mustang, never to be repeated. Earlier on in the model year, Ford saw the "ponycar war" handwriting on the wall, and made the decision to completely redesign the Mustang for 1967. Their car would need a fresh new look and more serious horsepower in order to compete with the new offerings coming from GM and Chrysler.

On Saturday, July 27, 1966, the Metuchen plant balanced out their 1966 Mustang production. Two days later, on Monday, July 29, San Jose rolled out their last cars. Dearborn would soldier on for another two weeks, finally wrapping it up on Friday, August 12. The 1966 model year saw a record production of 607,568 Mustangs.

Body and Exterior Trim

Nineteen sixty-six saw the continuation of the hardtop, convertible, and fastback body styles. The three basic configurations remained identical to the earlier cars, but several exterior trim changes occurred. The standard grille was now an "egg crate," extruded aluminum unit that featured chromed horizontal strips and a "floating" horse/corral emblem. On GT models, the bright horizontal

continued on page 100

Above: All 1966 Mustangs (except GTs and Accent Group cars) received the new "three forward thrusting bars" on their rear quarter panel air scoops. Rocker panel molding also became standard equipment. Left: The standard nonremote control sideview mirror was continued over for the 1966 model year.

The hot-selling GT package continued to sell like, well, hotcakes.

BODY SPECIFICATIONS

	Hardtop	Convertible	Fastback
Length (overall)	181.6″	181.6″	181.6″
Width (overall)	68.2″	68.2″	68.2″
Height (overall)	51.1″	51.0″	51.2″
Wheelbase	108.0″	108.0″	108.0″
Curb weight	2,610 lbs.	2,770 lbs.	2,640 lbs.
(Six-cyl., std. trans.)			

WARRANTY PLATE DECODING FOR 1966

ON THE VEHICLE WARRANTY NUMBER:

Assembly Plant Codes
F = Dearborn, MI
R = San Jose, CA
T = Metuchen, NJ

Body Serial Codes
07 = Hardtop Coupe
08 = Convertible
09 = Fastback

Engine Codes
A = 289-4V V-8 High Compression/Premium
   Fuel/Hydraulic Lifter
C = 289-2V V-8 Low Compression/Regular Fuel/Hydraulic
   Lifter
K = 289-2V V-8 High Performance/Premium
   Fuel/Mechanical Lifter
T = 200-1V Six Low Compression/Regular Fuel/Hydraulic
   Lifter

Consecutive Unit Number
The remaining six digits in the VIN indicate the vehicle's
consecutive unit number assigned at the production line.

ON THE LINE ABOVE THE VEHICLE WARRANTY NUMBER:

Body Style Codes
63A = Fastback/Standard Interior
65A = Hardtop Coupe/Standard Interior
76A = Convertible/Standard Interior
63B = Fastback/Interior Decor Group (Pony Interior)
65B = Hardtop Coupe/Interior Decor Group
76B = Convertible/Interior Decor Group
65C = Hardtop Coupe/Bench Seat
76C = Convertible/Bench Seat

Color Codes
A = Raven Black
F = Arcadian Blue
H = Sahara Beige
K = Nightmist Blue
M = Wimbledon White
P = Antique Bronze
R = Ivy Green Metallic
T = Candyapple Red Apple Red
U = Tahoe Turquoise
V = Emberglo
X = Vintage Burgundy
Y = Silver Blue
Z = Sauterne Gold
4 = Silver Frost
5 = Signalflare Red

8 = Springtime Yellow
I7 = Lime Gold (1967 Color)
Q7 = Brittany Blue (1967 Color)
Y7 = Dark Moss Green (1967 Color)
W7 = Clearwater Aqua (1967 Color)

Trim Codes
Standard Interior
22 = Blue
25 = Red
26 = Black
27 = Aqua
D2 = Parchment w/Blue Appointments
D3 = Parchment w/Burgundy Appointments
D4 = Parchment w/Emberglo Appointments
D6 = Parchment w/Black Appointments
D7 = Parchment w/Aqua Appointments
D8 = Parchment w/Ivy Gold Appointments
D9 = Parchment w/Palomino Appointments

Interior Decor Group (also known as a Pony interior)
62 = Blue/White
64 = Emberglo/Parchment
65 = Red
66 = Black
67 = Aqua/White
68 = Ivy Gold/White
F2 = Parchment w/Blue Appointments
F3 = Parchment w/Burgundy Appointments
F4 = Parchment w/Emberglo Appointments
F5 = Parchment w/Black Appointments
F7 = Parchment w/Aqua Appointments
F8 = Parchment w/Ivy Gold Appointments
F9 = Parchment w/Palomino Appointments

Bench Seat Interior
32 = Blue
35 = Red
36 = Black
C2 = Parchment w/Blue Appointments
C3 = Parchment w/Burgundy Appointments
C4 = Parchment w/Emberglo Appointments
C6 = Parchment w/Black Appointments
C7 = Parchment w/Aqua Appointments
C8 = Parchment w/Ivy Gold Appointments
C9 = Parchment w/Palomino Appointments

Date Codes
H = August 1965
J = September 1965
K = October 1965
L = November 1965
M = December 1965
A = January 1966
B = February 1966
C = March 1966
D = April 1966
E = May 1966
F = June 1966
G = July 1966
V = August 1966
Note: The number (1–31) that appears before the month
letter indicates the day.

DSO (District Sales Office)
Note: 1966 DSO codes were identical to 1965 DSOs from
August 1965 until the end of December. After production
began on January 1, 1966, DSO codes changed to the
following:
11 = Boston
13 = New York
15 = Newark

16 = Philadelphia
17 = Washington, D.C.
21 = Atlanta
22 = Charlotte
24 = Jacksonville
25 = Richmond
27 = Cincinnati
28 = Louisville
32 = Cleveland
33 = Detroit
34 = Indianapolis
35 = Lansing
37 = Buffalo
38 = Pittsburgh
41 = Chicago
42 = Fargo
43 = Milwaukee
44 = Twin Cities
45 = Davenport
51 = Denver
52 = Des Moines
53 = Kansas City
54 = Omaha
55 = St. Louis
61 = Dallas
62 = Houston
63 = Memphis
64 = New Orleans
65 = Oklahoma City
71 = Los Angeles
72 = San Jose
73 = Salt Lake City
74 = Seattle
75 = Phoenix
81 = Ford of Canada
83 = U.S. Government
84 = Home Office Reserve
85 = American Red Cross
89 = Transportation Services
90–99 = Export

Canadian District DSOs
Note: Canada's DSO list became effective on January 1,
1966. From August 1965 through December 1965, DSO
81 was used to indicate Mustangs that were for Cana-
dian export.
B1 = Central Canada
B2 = Eastern Canada
B3 = Atlantic Canada
B4 = Midwestern Canada
B6 = Western Canada
B7 = Pacific Canada

Axle Codes

CONVENTIONAL	LIMITED SLIP	AXLE RATIO
1	A	3.00:1
2	B	2.83:1
3	C	3.20:1
5	E	3.50:1
6	F	2.80:1
8	H	3.89:1
9	I	4.11:1

Transmission codes
1 = Three-Speed Manual (non-synchronized)
3 = Three Speed Manual (fully synchronized)
5 = Four-Speed Manual (all engines)
6 = C-4 Dual-Range Cruise-O-Matic

Far left: GT Mustangs got their own gas caps for 1966. Left: All cars continued to have their VINs stamped into the upper flange on the inner fender well.

Far left: The trunk of a 1966 convertible. Trunk mat design carried over unchanged for the 1966 model year. Left: The jacking instructions are positioned correctly on the inside of this trunk lid. That is to say, any way the person on the assembly line felt like! Below: Vinyl roofs were a $75 option on all first-generation Mustangs from 1964½ through 1966. They included a bright molding at the roof base.

For a compact car, the Mustang really was quite spacious on the inside.

For the standard interior for the 1966 models, all Mustangs came equipped with the five-gauge instrument panel layout. The centrally located round speedometer is flanked with fuel and oil gauges to the left, and ammeter and temperature gauges on the right.

Base equipment upholstery in the 1966 cars now featured knit-weave vinyl inserts in their center sections.

Inner door panel design changed as well to a horizontal pleat format surrounded by a bright chrome molding.

Continued from page 96
strips were blackened, providing a tougher-looking appearance. Dual fog lamps still dominated the GT's grille, and were fastened by two horizontal spikes similar to the 1965 model.

The bright hood lip molding on last year's GT was made standard fare on every Mustang, as were bright rocker panel moldings (deleted on GT) and reverse lights.

The new-for-1966 rear quarter panel air scoop design was best described by Ford: ". . . it features three forward thrusting bars to enhance Mustang's look of fleetness and motion."

Gas cap design changed for 1966. The ceramic center on previous years was nixed in favor of an extruded all-steel unit featuring the running horse and tricolored bars. GT cars received option-specific gas caps, with a large "GT" emblazoned in the center.

Body specifications remained identical to the 1965 models.

The actual warranty plate changed in design for 1966. All the pertinent info was still there, but the plate itself was slightly downsized.

Interior

Interior changes to the 1966 Mustang were about as extensive as the exterior changes; that is to say,

Above: The interior decor group carried over from the 1965 model year unchanged.

Right: The optional Rally-Pac tach and clock were carried over from the midyear 1965 version. The 1966 Rally-Pacs were available in a black finish or color-keyed to the steering column. Note that this particular version is calibrated to 6,000 rpm. K-code cars received 8,000-rpm tachometers.

Right: This particular pony interior" is equipped with a fairly rare lockable glove box door.

Far right: Just like the 1965 versions, 1966 pony interiors were available in monotone or two-tone color combinations. The galloping horses emblem was molded directly into the vinyl upholstery on both versions.

Above left and right: The spectacular pony interior (interior decor group) in Emberglo with Parchment Appointments.

Left: Inner door panels were totally different on Mustangs equipped with pony interiors. Note the pistol-grip door handle with woodgrain applique. The doors also came with a low-mounted courtesy light. Pony interior–equipped cars also received carpeted lower kick-panels (the small panels located underneath the instrument panel, near where you would rest your feet).

fairly minimal. All cars were fitted with the five-gauge instrument cluster as standard equipment. Mustangs sporting the pony interior still received the woodgrain dash look, while all other cars were treated to camera-case black. All speedometers, regardless of engine size, were now marked to 140 miles per hour.

The dash pad was revised slightly for 1966 with more pronounced "pods" on both the driver and passenger sides.

Interior door panel design changed from the earlier vertical pleat motif to a horizontal pleat format.

Standard seats on 1966 Mustangs received knit-weave vinyl inserts in their center sections, while the earlier versions were made entirely of smooth-grained vinyl.

The full bench seat was once again an option for 1966. Like the 1965 version, it was not available with the deluxe interior group.

Interior color choices were down slightly from 1965. "Only" 34 colors and combinations were available for 1966, but it was still a far cry from the Mustang's initial offering of 12!

Padded sun visors became a standard item on all cars, as did rear seat belts. All seat belts were now color-keyed.

As a carryover feature from the earlier cars, convertible Mustangs featured a manually oper-ated top that was designed with counterbalanced springs to provide easy operation of the relatively lightweight roof. An electrohydraulic power–operated top was optional.

The "all Corporate Blue" 200-ci inline six.

Chassis

The Falcon-derived platform chassis remained unchanged for the 1966 production year. All three body styles (hardtop, convertible, and fastback) rode on the same basic setup.

As described in chapter 3, convertible Mustangs were equipped with "torque boxes" and additional all-steel reinforcements to provide proper chassis rigidity.

Regardless of engine size (six or eight cylinders), all Mustangs were based on the same platform chassis. Upgraded suspension components were used to compensate for the weight and power differences associated with the optional V-8 engines.

Engines

200-1V

Nineteen sixty-six brought two fairly substantial changes to Ford's entire engine lineup. The most obvious change was the decision to paint all engines a medium dark blue color, which became known as Ford Corporate Blue. Not only were the engine blocks painted this color, but the valve covers and air cleaners were as well.

BASE EQUIPMENT ENGINE: T-CODE

Type:	Six-cylinder, inline, overhead valve
Displacement:	200 cubic inches
Foundry group:	Fairlane "Six"
Bore and stroke:	3.68x3.13
Maximum compression ratio: (with standard gaskets)	9.2:1
Gross horsepower at 4,400 rpm:	120
Gross torque at 2,400 rpm:	190 ft.lbs.
Valve lifters:	Hydraulic
Carburetor:	Autolite 1100, 1V
Recommended fuel:	Regular
Emission controls CA only:	Thermactor
Emission controls 49 states:	N/A
Dimensions:	33"L x 33"W x 28"H
Weight:	360 lbs.

The other big news for 1966 was the emission control standards passed by the California legislature, which went into effect January 1, 1966. For California DSO Mustangs, Ford decided to meet these new requirements right from the start of their 1966 model production. The smog controls, as they quickly became known, employed an air pump that injected air directly into the cylinder head exhaust passages. At this point, the additional

Above: The Limited Edition 200 Sprint was just a dressed-up appearance package for both the car and the engine. The car received the accent appearance group, wire wheel covers, center console, and numerous smaller upgrades, and the engine came with a "dress-up" kit that included a chrome air cleaner, chrome valve cover, and a Sprint 200 decal. The engine's mechanicals were identical to the base 200. Left: Air and gas were sucked in through the Autolite 1100 one-barrel carburetor equipped with an automatic choke.

Right: The single exhaust system for six-cylinder cars was virtually identical to the 1964½ and 1965 cars.

Below: For this 289 two-barrel C-code for 1966, the modified "tap" on its air-conditioning connection is not stock; neither are the gray colored sparkplug wires. All plug wires should be black.

oxidation of combusted air and gas reduced the level of contaminates expelled into the atmosphere.

The smog control system involved excessive "plumbing." Hoses ran alongside the engine and across the front of the air cleaner, without appearing very orderly under the hood. The air pump even required a special cast-iron mount that displaced the alternator to a new lower position. Of course, this rearranging necessitated the need for new mounting brackets for both the air pump and the alternator. Many other minor engine modifications were required due to the implementation of the new smog laws, mostly adjustments made to castings to accept the new system. *Bob Mannel's Mustang & Ford Small Block V-8, Volumes 1 and 2,* covers in great detail all of the revisions made to 1966 engines due to the new smog laws.

Other than the revisions already listed, the inline 200-ci six-cylinder remained unchanged for the 1966 model year.

(For a complete description of the color schemes associated with 1966 engines, please see chapter 1.)

Exhaust

The single exhaust system used for 1965 production model 200s was carried over for 1966.

289-2V

The 289-2V and 4V engines received changes to their valve trains in September 1965. Affecting the 1966 model cars, this change replaced all the valves, springs, and spring retainers. The new valves remained the same length as before, but the valve spring retainer groove was located slightly lower on the valve stem. To make things equal, the new valve springs were equally shorter in height, and the springs were smaller in diameter.

OPTIONAL EQUIPMENT ENGINE: C-CODE	
Type:	Eight-cylinder, 90-degree V, overhead valve
Displacement:	289 cubic inches
Foundry group:	Fairlane V8
Bore and stroke:	4.00x2.87
Maximum compression ratio: (with standard gaskets)	9.3:1
Gross horsepower at 4,400 rpm:	200
Gross torque at 2,400 rpm:	282 ft.-lbs.
Valve lifters:	Hydraulic
Carburetor:	Autolite 2100, 2V
Recommended fuel:	Regular
Emission controls CA only:	Thermactor
Emission controls 49 states:	N/A
Dimensions:	28"L x 25"W x 29"H
Weight:	460 lbs.

The 289 A-code four-barrel small block. This particular engine was built in late June 1966, very close to the end of model year production. Note the taller-than-usual valve covers. They were actually the new-for-1967 design. We found no explanation for this difference other than as Ford was winding down 1966 production, it probably ran out of the "correct" valve covers. Strange but true!

The engine on this particular 1966 K-code 289-4V (right) has been treated to several dealer-added accessories that were available in 1966 through selected Ford dealerships: Cobra-style finned valve covers, a special intake manifold, special tri-power carburetor setup, and a Cobra-style high-performance air cleaner. The term tri-power refers to the three two-barrel carburetors (below), offering increased air-flow. The stock K-code 289 received chrome valve covers and a circular chrome open-element air cleaner similar to the K-code photos pictured in chapter 4. Of course, the engine block and major adjoining assemblies were painted Ford Corporate Blue for the 1966 model year.

OPTIONAL EQUIPMENT ENGINE: A-CODE

Type:	Eight-cylinder, 90-degree V, overhead valve
Displacement:	289 cubic inches
Foundry group:	Fairlane V8
Bore and stroke:	4.00x2.87
Maximum compression ratio: (with standard gaskets)	9.8:1
Gross horsepower at 4,800 rpm:	225
Gross torque at 3,200 rpm:	305 ft.-lbs.
Valve lifters:	Hydraulic
Carburetor:	Autolite 4100, 4V
Recommended fuel:	Premium
Emission controls CA only:	Thermactor
Emission controls 49 states:	N/A
Dimensions:	28"L x 25"W x 29"H
Weight:	465 lbs.

OPTIONAL EQUIPMENT ENGINE: K-CODE

Type:	Eight-cylinder, 90-degree V, overhead valve
Displacement:	289 cubic inches
Foundry group:	Fairlane V8
Bore and stroke:	4.00x2.87
Maximum compression ratio: (with standard gaskets)	10.5:1
Gross horsepower at 6,000 rpm:	271
Gross torque at 3,400 rpm:	312 ft.-lbs.
Valve lifters:	Solid/adjustable
Carburetor:	Autolite 4100, 4V
Recommended fuel:	Super Premium
Emission controls CA only:	Thermactor
Emission controls 49 states:	N/A
Dimensions:	28"L x 25"W x 29"H
Weight:	465 lbs.

These types of revisions were known as "level changes," a fairly common occurrence throughout the model years. They were mostly implemented to standardize parts and procedures, and to minimize costs.

A fairly significant 1966 change affecting both C-code and A-code engines involved the switch from conventional-type rockers to a rail-type design. Because of this change, the pushrod holes in the cylinder heads could be opened up. Previously, the valve train's alignment was maintained by the pushrods moving through the close-tolerance holes in the cylinder heads. Now, with the rail-type rocker arms, alignment was dependent on the arms maintaining position over the extended valve stem tips. This particular revision was referred to as "change level 11."

Like the rest of the engine lineup for 1966, the 289-2V was painted Ford Corporate Blue, and California-bound C-codes received the new smog controls. Cars for the other 49 states were unaffected.

Exhaust
The 1966 289-2V single exhaust system was virtually identical to its 1965 predecessor.

289-4V
As mentioned in the 289-2V section, the 289-4V underwent identical changes to its valve train in 1966. Engine performance levels were unaffected.

The 289-4V also received a coat of Ford Corporate Blue on its block, valve covers, and air cleaner. California DSO A-codes were equipped with smog controls. Cars for the other 49 states were unaffected.

Exhaust
Dual exhaust, similar to the Hi-Performance 289's, was now standard equipment on A-code engines for 1966. The single exhaust system used on 1965 A-code Mustangs was no longer available.

289-4V "Hi-Po"
When the Fairlane 390 big block was introduced in various intermediate and full-size applications for 1966, Ford's other car lines no longer needed the "hi-po." Suddenly, the legendary Hi-Performance 289 became sole property of the Mustang.

The valve train revisions that affected the 289-2V and 4V engines did not affect the K-code engine due to the valve lash requirements of the hi-po's mechanical camshaft.

Ford Corporate Blue paint graced the hi-po's engine as well, but the valve covers and free-flow air cleaner remained highly polished chrome. Other than the addition of smog controls on California K-codes, the most potent engine in the Mustang's arsenal remained untouched for 1966.

Exhaust
The exhaust system remained unchanged from its revised-for-1965 setup.

Transmissions

With an engine lineup that remained unchanged for 1966, so did the transmission offerings. The only exception was the addition of a second version of the Cruise-O-Matic, and its availability not only on the 289-2V and 4V, but on the Hi-Performance K-code as well.

With the exception of the K-code engines, all V-8–powered Mustangs came standard with the constant-mesh, fully synchronized three-speed transmission as standard equipment.

CONVENTIONAL SIX-CYLINDER THREE-SPEED MANUAL GEAR RATIOS

First	2.76:1
Second	1.69:1
Third	1.00:1
Reverse	3.74:1

The Cruise-O-Matic transmission actually was available in three different gear ratio configurations, but only two of them pertained to the Mustang. Some excerpts from Ford's dealer brochures described the feature: ". . . Vacuum-controlled automatic shifting provides velvet-smooth gear changes for any driving condition. For normal driving, positioning Cruise-O-Matic in D (green dot) will start the transmission in first gear. The vacuum control will then take over, tailoring upshifts to driver demand and engine torque. If faster than normal acceleration is called for, the vacuum control will delay shifting, utilizing engine power to maximum advantage. Also, vacuum control allows downshifting to second gear during the passing maneuver without the necessity for full throttle, providing a quick, smooth shift without over-revving the engine."

Clutches

Clutch design and configuration remained unchanged throughout the 1966 model year. Six-cylinder cars used noncentrifugal clutches, while eight-cylinder Mustangs used semicentrifugal units.

All clutches on manual transmission Mustangs were a single-disc, dry plate configuration.

Rear Axles

Six-Cylinder Models

Rear axle/differential design and assembly were unchanged from the previous year. Base Mustangs equipped with six-cylinder engines used a solid cast-iron axle housing. An offset drive pinion was supported by two tapered roller bearings positioned ahead of the ring gear. The axle shafts were made from induction-hardened steel forgings with cold-rolled splines at the ends that connected to the differential and wheel hub flanges at the outer ends.

Eight-Cylinder Models

Also unchanged from the 1964½ and 1965 assemblies, eight-cylinder Mustangs featured a rear axle with a straddle-mounted pinion and a banjo-type housing. This configuration provided bearing support on both sides of the pinion, keeping the pinion and ring gear in a constant alignment. V-8 differentials featured two tapered roller bearings located ahead of the pinion gear and a straight roller bearing located behind the gear to provide excellent support for the pinion shaft, in both front and back. The individual axles were made from induction-hardened steel forgings with cold-rolled splines that connected with the differential and wheel hub flanges at the outer ends.

CONVENTIONAL V8 CONSTANT MESH THREE-SPEED MANUAL GEAR RATIOS

First	2.79:1
Second	1.70:1
Third	1.00:1
Reverse	2.87:1

FOUR-SPEED MANUAL TRANSMISSION GEAR RATIOS (SIX-CYLINDER)

First	3.16:1
Second	2.21:1
Third	1.41:1
Fourth	1.00:1
Reverse	3.34:1

FOUR-SPEED MANUAL TRANSMISSION GEAR RATIOS (289-2V, 4V, AND 289-4V HI-PERFORMANCE)

	289-2V, 4V	289-4V "hi-po"
First	2.78:1	2.32:1
Second	1.93:1	1.69:1
Third	1.36:1	1.29:1
Fourth	1.00:1	1.00:1
Reverse	2.78:1	2.32:1

CRUISE-O-MATIC GEAR RATIOS TYPE 1 (AVAILABLE ON ALL ENGINES EXCEPT 289-4V HI-PERFORMANCE)

First	2.46:1
Second	1.46:1
Third	1.00:1
Reverse	2.20:1

CRUISE-O-MATIC GEAR RATIOS TYPE 2 (AVAILABLE ON ALL V8 ENGINES, STANDARD ON 289-4V HI-PERFORMANCE)

First	2.40:1
Second	1.47:1
Third	1.00:1
Reverse	2.00:1

AXLE BUILD TAGS

Tag#	Diameter	Ratio	Type	Application Notes
WCY-E	7.25"	3.20	Conventional, 2 pin	With 200 engine and manual transmission
WCY-L	7.25"	3.20	Equa lock, 2 pin	With 200 engine and manual transmission
WCY-R	7.25"	2.83	Conventional, 2 pin	With 200 engine and automatic transmission
WCY-AA	7.25"	2.83	Equa lock, 2 pin	With 200 engine and automatic transmission
WCY-AJ	7.25"	3.20	Conventional, 2 pin	With 200 engine and automatic transmission
WCZ-R	8.75"	3.89	Conventional, 2 pin	High-performance applications only
WCZ-S	8.75"	3.50	Conventional, 2 pin	High-performance applications only
WCZ-T	8.75"	3.50	Equa lock, 2 pin	High-performance applications only

(For all other tags, see 1965 listings.)

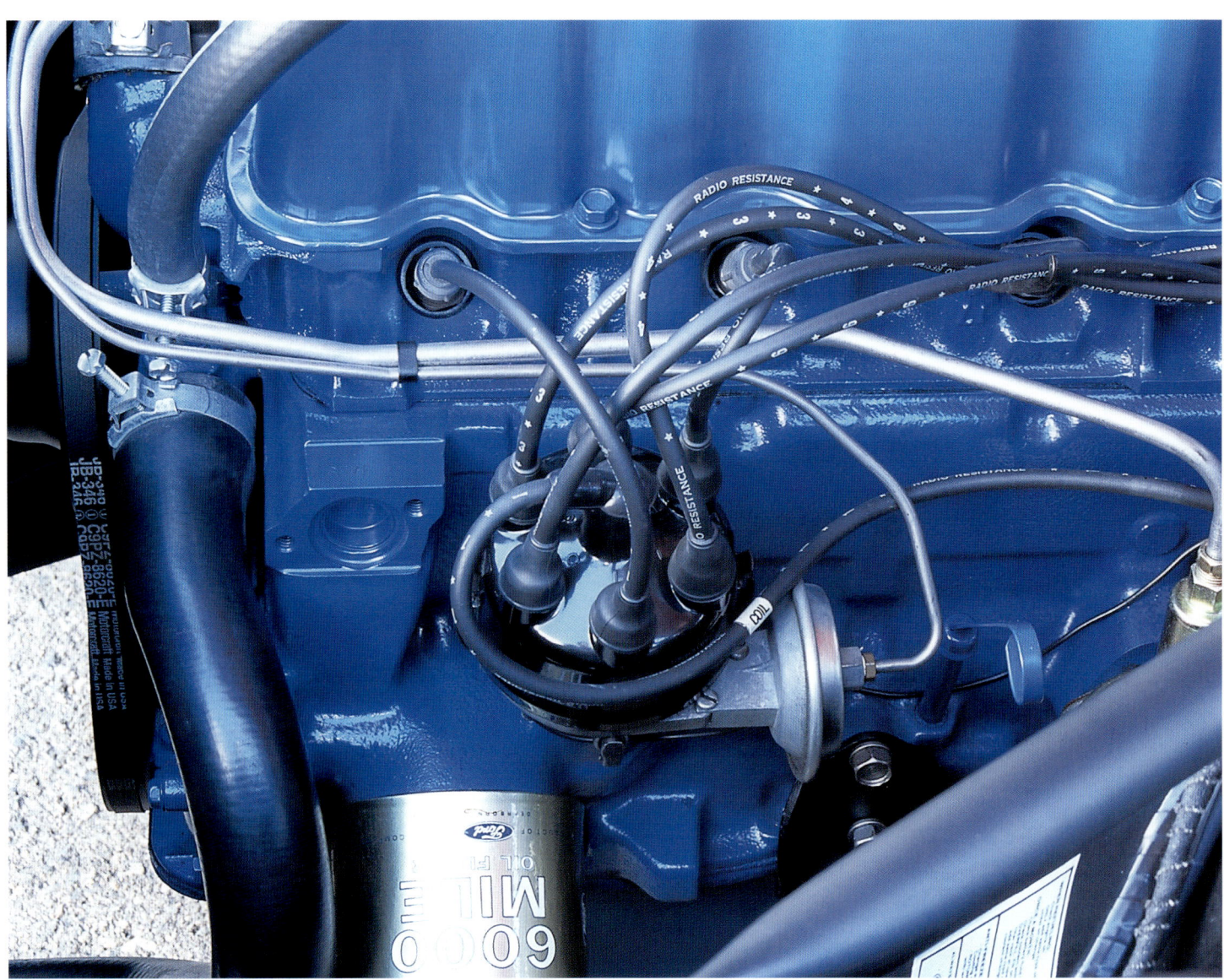

Both six- and eight-cylinder cars had an identification tag attached to the differential housing at the point of assembly. In chapter 1, we covered the decoding of an axle's build tag. The table on page 109 will further identify the differential type and the unit's application. Note that the applications were a little more varied and defined in 1966. Many 1965 units carried over to the 1966 model year.

Driveshaft and Universal Joints

All cars featured an exposed driveshaft with universal joints at either end. The driveshafts were made with seamless steel tubing that provided maximum strength and little added weight. Forged yokes were welded on at both ends, then the unit was precision balanced. Universal joints were the cross-and-yoke type, featuring sealed, prelubricated needle bearings. Service was required at 36,000-mile intervals.

Suspension, Steering, Brakes

Suspension systems on 1966 model year Mustangs were identical to the 1964½ and 1965 cars. As before, the heavy-duty suspension system came as standard equipment with the 289 Hi-Performance V-8 and on cars equipped with the GT package. It was optional on all other Mustangs equipped with a V-8 engine.

Steering

The steering systems (both manual and power) for 1966 were carried over unaltered from the early 1964½ and 1965 cars. Both six-cylinder and V-8 Mustangs were equipped with a parallelogram linkage–type steering system that used a cross-link and idler arm setup. The steering gear was a recirculating ball-and-nut type, identified by the trademark "Magic Circle." All friction points within the steering linkage were permanently lubricated, and the steering box (and gear) were filled with a life-of-car lubricant.

Six-cylinder distributors were mounted on the side of the engine block. Photo shows correct plug wire color and routing.

BRAKE SPECIFICATIONS

	Six-Cylinder	Eight-Cylinder
Brake drum diameter:	9 in.	10 in.
Lining material:	Molded asbestos	
Lining attachment:	Riveted	
Total lining area (sq. in.):	131.0	154.2

STEERING SPECIFICATIONS

Linkage:	Parallelogram with cross-link and idler arm
Gear type:	"Magic Circle" recirculating ball
Overall steering ratio:	
Manual	27:1
Power	22:1
Turns (lock to lock):	
Manual	4.5
Power	3.7
Turning diameter:	38.9 feet

Steering gear box build tags

1966	Tag ID
Manual steering (standard):	HCC-AT
Manual steering (performance):	HCC-AX
Power steering:	HCC-AW

The optional power steering system is proportional in design. Maximum steering effort required to activate the full power assist is 4 pounds of pressure. The power steering pump and reservoir were located near the front of the engine compartment, off to the left side of the motor. The special handling package and the power steering option (by itself) both offered the quicker gear ratio (22:1).

Brakes

Both six- and eight-cylinder 1966 Mustangs were equipped with the same braking system as the 1964½ and 1965 models. The standard drum-type brakes were single-anchor, self-energizing, internal expanding, and air-cooled.

The hydraulics of the Mustang's braking system utilized a jar-type cap and a diaphragm-type gasket that sealed the system against the outside elements.

The air conditioner's control center was located underneath the center of the instrument panel. The 1966 air conditioners received a black finish control panel.

The parking/emergency brake was conventional in design, and was engaged by a twist-and-release handle located under the left side of the instrument panel.

Optional front disc brakes could be ordered on 1966 Mustangs equipped with V-8 engines. The brakes incorporated a cast-iron disc with a brake pad on either side. Each brake pad was actuated by two brake cylinders. The disc was a one-piece casting with radial ribs separating the two sides of the disc, allowing air circulation for maximum heat dissipation. The rear brakes remained as a traditional drum setup.

Power-assisted brakes remained an option in 1966, but could not be ordered if disc brakes were specified. The vacuum-operated power booster was manufactured by Bendix and also by Midland Ross on 1966 model Mustangs. Presumably, Midland Ross was brought in to help meet the unprecedented demand. Bendix units featured an adjustable pushrod with tolerances between .980 inch and .995 inch, while Midland Ross pushrods could be adjusted from .995 inch to 1.50 inches.

Electrical, Cooling, Heating

Mustang's alternator-based charging system was carried over unaltered through the 1966 model year. The improved 12-volt electrical system teamed with a 38-ampere alternator provided the juice for all base-equipment Mustangs. The A-code and K-code cars used 42-amp alternators, as did those equipped with air conditioning.

The "improved-for-1965" standard battery was also carried over to the 1966 cars, and the optional heavy-duty, 55-ampere battery was available at a suggested retail price of $7.44.

Radiator capacity was improved for 1966. The six-cylinder cars began using 9½-quart units, and V-8–powered cars featured upgraded 14.5-quart versions. As before, both radiators were fully pressurized and regulated by thermostats located at the upper engine outlet on both six-cylinder and V-8 Mustangs.

Air-conditioned Mustangs continued to use five-bladed fans, and non-air-conditioned cars used four-bladed versions. Both fan styles were mounted to a stamped-steel engine pulley.

Optional airconditioning units were produced by Ford and were mounted directly under the center of the instrument panel. On 1966 cars, the face of the air conditioner was painted black and featured four circular bezels to direct airflow. The fan featured three speeds: High (6.5–7.5 amps), Medium (4.5–5.5 amps), and Low (3–4 amps). All air-conditioner compressors were located near the front of the engine and were typical belt-driven units. Air conditioning circuit protection was provided by a 3AG 15-amp fuse.

Carried over unchanged for the 1966 model year, Mustang heaters were located underneath the passenger side of the instrument panel and used water heated and circulated from the engine to operate. Blower motors featured three fan speeds: High (6–8 amps), Medium (4–6 amps), and Low (2-4 amps). The heater/blower used a circuit protector with a SFE 14-amp fuse.

Wheels and Tires

All Mustangs (both six- and eight-cylinders) received 14-inch wheels as standard equipment for the 1966 model year. As before, the wheels on the six-cylinder employed a four-lug pattern, and the wheels for the V-8 were five-lug. The special handling package continued on as an option for all eight-cylinder cars and as standard equipment for the K-code Mustangs.

The 1966 Mustangs (both six- and eight-cylinder versions) came standard with 6.95"x14" four-ply rayon black sidewall tires. High-grade nylon tires and white sidewall versions were optional. Once again, the dual red line tires were offered as standard equipment on the K-code cars, and were optional on all other Mustangs equipped with V-8 engines.

WHEEL SPECIFICATIONS

	Six-Cylinder	Eight-Cylinder
Type:	Stamped-steel ventilated disc with safety-type rims	
Number of studs:	4	5
Diameter and rim size:	14"x4.5"	14"x5"

TIRE SPECIFICATIONS

	6.95" x14"	6.95" x14"	6.95" x14"
6-cyl.	std.	opt.	-
8-cyl.	std.	opt.	opt.
8-cyl.*	-	opt.**	std.

*with handling package
** a no cost option tire, available in black or white sidewall

Although all wheels for 1966 were now 14-inch, the six-cylinder versions were still four-lug. Tire shown above is not original equipment. The standard wheel cover for all Mustangs (below) was now 14-inch.

Above: This optional wheel cover featured a knock-off style center cap.

The optional wire wheel cover for 14-inch applications was carried over from the 1965 model year.

Optional styled steel wheels were similar to the version introduced on 1965 models. The 1966 wheel featured an outer trim ring made of stainless steel.

OPTIONS

Taken directly from the dealer's suggested retail price listings, the following list indicates the optional equipment lineup for 1966. Most of the pricing was identical to the 1965 options list. We were not able to locate suggested retail pricing for the dealer-installed options. We suspect, however, that they too were similar to 1965. Note that the 271-HP V-8 was referred to as the Cobra engine.

Base Price:
2-Door Hardtop:	$2,416.18
Convertible:	$2,652.86
2+2 Fastback:	$2,607.07

Engines:
- 8-Cylinder 289-CID 2V 200-HP — $105.63
(extra charge over 200-CID 1V 120-HP six-cylinder)
- 8-Cylinder 289-CID 4V 225-HP — $52.85
(extra charge over 289-CID 2V)
- 8-Cylinder 289-CID 4V 271-HP Hi-Performance "Cobra" — $327.92
(extra charge over 289-CID 2V, includes Special Handling Package and 6.95x14 Dual Red Band Nylon Tires) N/A with GT Equip Group.
- With GT Equipment Group — $276.34

Transmissions:
- Cruise-O-Matic Six-Cylinder — $175.80
- Cruise-O-Matic 200/225-HP V-8s — $185.39
- Cruise-O-Matic V8 271-HP Hi-Performance Engine — $216.27
- Four-Speed Manual Six-Cylinder — $113.45
- Four-Speed Manual V-8 — $184.02

Power Assists:
- Power Brakes — $42.29
- Power Steering — $84.47
- Power Top, Convertible — $52.95

Comfort/Convenience Equipment:
- Air Conditioner, Ford — $310.90
(tinted glass recommended)
- AM Radio, Stereosonic Tape System (radio required) — $128.29
- Front Seat, Full with Arm Rest (hardtop and convertible) — $24.42
- Luggage Rack, Rear Deck Lid (hardtop and convertible) — $32.44
- Radio and Antenna — $57.51

Appearance Equipment:
- Accent Stripe, Less Rear Quarter Ornamentation — $13.90
- Console, Full Length — $50.41
- Console (for use with air conditioner) — $31.52
- Steering Wheel, Deluxe (simulated woodgrain) — $32.20
- Interior Decor Group — $94.13
(includes special interior trim, deluxe woodgrain steering wheel, R/W door courtesy lights and pistol-grip door handle)
- Vinyl Roof (hardtop) — $74.36
- Wire Wheel Covers — $58.24
- Wheel Covers w/Knock-Off Hubs — $19.48

Special Equipment:
- Closed Crankcase Emission System (available only — $5.19
with exhaust ECS except with 271-HP engines)
- Exhaust Emission Control System N/A with 271-HP Engine — $45.45

Delete Options:
- Magic Aire Heater — ($31.52)

Performance Equipment:
- Disc Brakes, Front, Eight-cylinder (N/A with power brakes) — $56.77
- Limited Slip Differential — $41.60
- Rally Pac w/Clock/Tachometer — $69.30
- Special Handling Package, 200- and 225-HP V8 Engines — $30.64
(includes increased-rate front and rear springs, larger front and rear shock absorbers, 22:1 steering ratio, and larger-diameter front stabilizer bar)
- GT Equipment Group — $152.20
(available with 225- and 271-HP V-8 engines only: includes dual exhaust system with bright extensions through valance panel, Special Handling Package components, disc brakes, fog lamps and grille bar, GT stripe, GT ornamentation, less rocker panel molding)
- Wheels, Styled Steel 14 inch (V-8 only) — $93.84
- Battery, Heavy-Duty, 55 amps

Safety Equipment:
- Electric Windshield Wipers, 2 Speed — $12.95
- Deluxe Seat Belts, Front and Rear (front retractors) — $14.53
and Warning Light
- Visibility Group (includes remote control mirror, day/nite mirror, 2-speed electric wipers) — $29.81
- Glass, Tinted with Banded Windshield — $30.25
- Windshield Only, Tinted and Banded — $21.09

Optional Tire Prices:
Five 6.95x14 BSW Rayon tires were standard equipment on all models except those equipped with the 271-HP Hi-Performance engine.
Extra charge for:
- 6.95x14 WSW — $33.31
- 6.95x14 BSW, Nylon — $15.67
- 6.95x14 WSW, Nylon — $48.89
- 6.95x14 Dual Red Band, Nylon — $48.97

Five 6.95x14 Dual Red Band Nylon tires were standard equipment on all models with the 271-HP Hi-Performance engine.
No extra charge for:
- 6.95x14 BSW Nylon — N/C
- 6.95x14 WSW Nylon — N/C

Dealer-Installed Accessories:
- Air Conditioner
- Air Horns
- Armrests, Rear (Hardtop)
- Battery, Heavy-Duty, 55 amps
- Brakes, Power
- Cigarette Lighter
- Clothes Rod
- Compass
- Door Edge Guards
- Door Sill Plate
- Door Storage Compartment (Black Only)
- Engine Coolant Heater 550-, or 1,000-watt
- Engine Performance and Dress-Up Kits (Cobra, All V-8 Engines)
- Fire Extinguisher, 2- or 5-lbs. Dry Chemical
- Floor Mats, Rubber or Vinyl, Front or Rear
- Frame, License Plate
- Gas Cap, Locking
- Glove Compartment and Console Door Lock
- Lake Pipes
- Light, Engine/Trunk Compartment
- Light, Rear Seat (Hardtop and Convertible)
- Light, Parking Brake Warning
- Limited Slip Differential
- Lighter, 12-volt Map Lite
- Litter Basket
- Luggage Rack Kit, Rear Deck Mount (Hardtop and Convertible)
- Luggage Rack Kit, Roof Mount (Hardtop)
- Mirrors
  - Inside Nonglare, Day/Nite
  - Outside Rearview, Circular
  - Outside Rearview, Remote Control (Matching RH nonremote mirror also available)
- Racing Stripes, Red, White, Blue
- Radiator Insect Screen
- Radio, Transistorized, AM Pushbutton, Antenna Included
- Radios and Antennas, Two-Way Citizen's Band
- Radio Speaker, Rear, Conventional and Studiosonic (Hardtop)
- Rally-Pac w/Clock/Tachometer Combination
- Reflector Flare Kit
- Seat Belt Retractors
- Seat, Child, Safety
- Seat Cushion, Ventilated
- Ski Rack Kits (Hardtop and Convertible)
- Spotlight
- Steering, Power
- Steering Wheel, Deluxe
- Stereosonic Tape System, Under Panel Mount
- Tachometers, 6,000- and 9,000-rpm
- Tire Chains
- Tissue Dispenser
- Tonneau Cover (Convertible)
- Tool Kit
- Trunk Release, Remote
- Turn Signals, Fender Mounted
- Vacuum Cleaner, 12 volts
- Wheel Covers, Deluxe w/Knock-Off Hubs
- Wheel Covers, Simulated Wire
- Wheels, Styled Steel (All V-8 Models)
- Wheel Trim Rings

Pony "bumperettes" were an aftermarket dealer-installed accessory.

Chapter 6

The Shelby Mustangs

Even though the new Mustangs were smashing every sales record imaginable, the good folks at Ford could already see a giant cloud looming on the horizon. No one launches a massive strike against the enemy then sits back expecting nothing to happen. The Mustang's success really did catch GM and Chrysler by surprise, but it would only be a matter of time before somebody tried to one-up the new kid on the block. Chevrolet already had their Corvette, which boasted a

375-horsepower fuel-injected engine in 1964. Pontiac had just introduced their Tempest line's latest option: a 389-ci fire-breathing monster called GTO. Worse still, by August 1964 word was out that GM and Chrysler were already planning cars that would go head-to-head against Mustang for a piece of the ponycar pie. For Ford, it was time to get moving again, and quickly.

Carroll Shelby had been busy converting AC's Ace sports cars into mind-blowing rocketships by

This modified 1965 Shelby is ready to take on the mean streets.

The incredible 1965 Shelby GT-350 in the late afternoon sun, overlooking the Pacific Ocean.

stuffing them full of 289 Blue Oval power. This modification proved to be immensely successful, as the almost-defunct Aces were winning every race they entered. With Shelby's record for doing it right, he attracted the attention of the Ford Motor Company. In a meeting with Lee Iacocca, Carroll Shelby listened as Iacocca complained about getting nowhere with the Sports Car Club of America (SCCA). In its zeal to ward off the upcoming storm of competition, Ford had tried to get the Mustang recognized as a production racecar for SCCA competition in the United States. The SCCA wasn't buying it. Carroll, however, was personally acquainted with John Bishop, who just

happened to be the executive director of the SCCA. The Iacocca-Shelby meeting ended with Shelby telling Iacocca he would talk to John Bishop about Ford's little dilemma.

After a meeting with Bishop and a little soul searching, Shelby came back to Iacocca with the news: In order to qualify the Mustang for SCCA status, the car would have to be converted into a two-seater. The SCCA's other stipulation was that either the car's suspension or the engine could be modified, but not both. Shelby also related that they would need 100 of these cars ready by January 1, 1965, to be race "eligible" that year. It was the old homologation rule that racing organizations

Above and opposite: Super-rare, one of six 1966 Shelby GT-350 convertibles in Springtime Yellow (paint code 8). *Photo by Tom Shaw*

impose. Shelby and Iacocca sat down and devised a plan.

By taking on this project, Shelby initially thought he might have a problem on his hands. Selling 100 pure racecars might be a losing proposition. Then he came to the realization that he could produce two versions of the car: one would be specifically designed for racing, the other would be a little more toned down for street use.

Ford would have no problem cranking out the cars. They would all come from the San Jose manufacturing plant and be shipped to Shelby's newly rented manufacturing facilities near the airport in Los Angeles. Shelby would gain a great deal of

new business, and Ford would introduce the first "muscle Mustang" to the mean streets. As it was now called, the new Cobra-Mustang program was immediately approved by Ford.

Shelby American's competition director and development driver Ken Miles was put to the task. They supplied him with two hardtop Mustangs and a bunch of Ford High-Performance Parts books, then sent him to the Willow Springs Raceway. Miles's objective was to piece together a Mustang that would exhibit extraordinary handling characteristics on the racetrack, and still maintain a reasonable level of streetability. As a little added challenge, this new package had to

include economical parts that were readily available from Ford. No small job! Success eventually came with a little help from Ford chassis engineer Klaus Arning and Shelby team co-driver Bob Bondurant.

The next step for Shelby was ordering three stock Wimbledon White Mustang fastbacks. One was to be the first street Shelby prototype and the other two were allotted for race duty. The three cars were taken out to Willow Springs for extensive testing. After all the details and adjustments were finally ironed out, Shelby American was ready for assembly-line production.

All the 1965 model Shelbys were Wimbledon White (paint code M). Shelby American ordered them from Ford as special-order stripped-down cars, meaning they came from the factory with no hoods or hood latches, no grille, radio, seat belts, rear seats, exhaust system, quarter panel ornamentation, or emblems. They all came into Shelby with black interiors, 8.75-inch rear ends,

four-speed manual transmissions, and the 271-horsepower 289-ci K-code engine.

As legend has it, the name GT-350 was coined in a totally random incident. After wrestling with numerous variations of Cobra and various number/letter combinations relating to engine size, the potential legal ramifications were getting out of hand. Seems one day Carroll Shelby looked out across the street and asked his chief engineer

The amazing-but-true 1966 Shelby GT-350H. Ford/Shelby–built 936 specially prepped for the Hertz rental car company. The Hertz cars were equipped with special Magnum 500–styled steel wheels.

BODY SPECIFICATIONS (FASTBACK)

Length (overall)	181.6"
Width (overall)	68.2"
Height (overall)	
1965	49.6" (approx. street version)
1966	51.1"
Wheelbase	108.0"
Curb weight	
1965	2,490 lbs. (approx., street version)
1966	2,620 lbs.

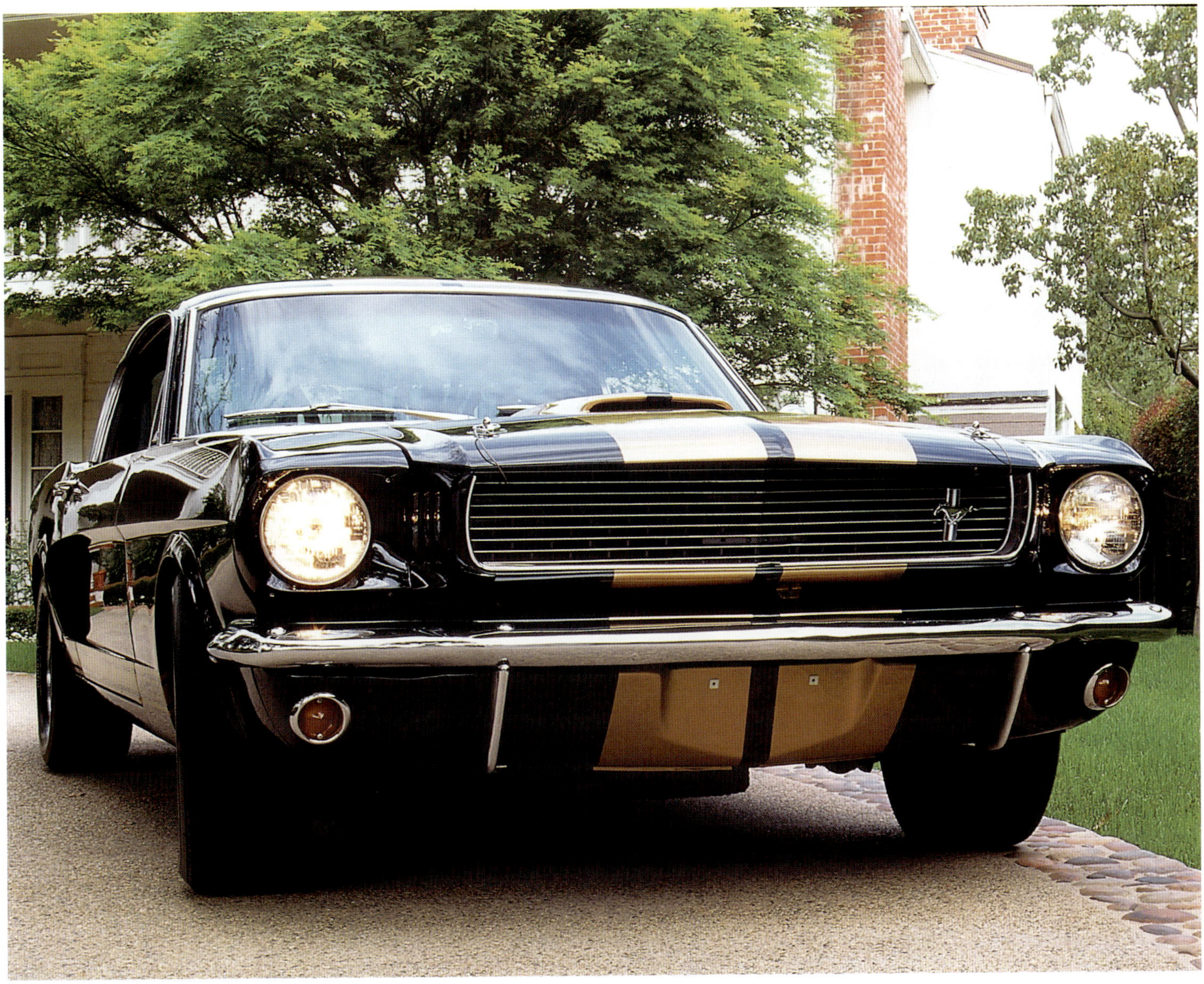

G.T. 350
CALIFORNIA
2WHL 650

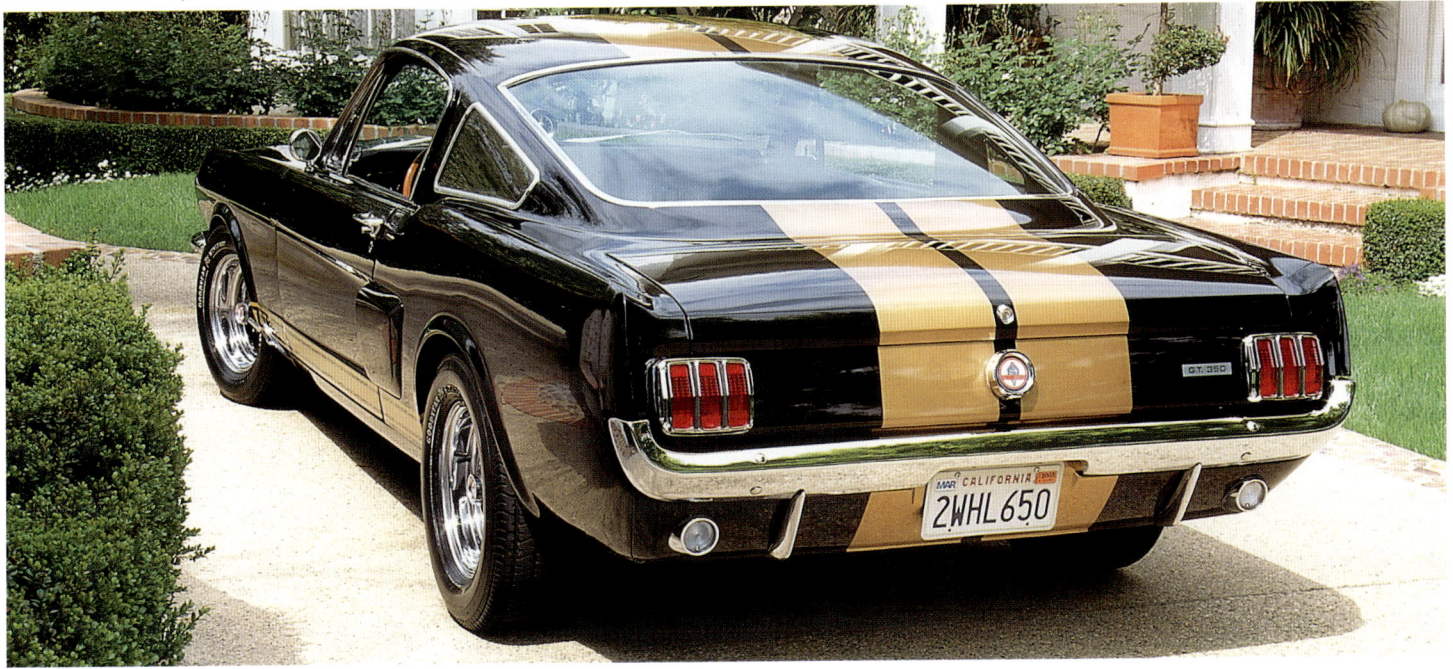

Phil Remington how far away he thought a building was from where they sat. After they both guessed at the distance, Remington actually went outside and paced off the distance. "Three hundred and fifty feet" was his answer. "Fine" said Shelby. "Let's call the little car the GT-350. If the car's good, the name won't matter, and if it's no good, the name won't matter."

Between the car's inception and the end of 1965 Mustang production, Shelby American managed to crank out 562 street GT-350s. The racing version went on to fame and fortune, literally dominating a class made up of Ferraris, Corvettes, Jaguars, Mercedes, and Lotuses. In fact, the Shelby GT-350s went on to win the SCCA "B Class" National Championship in 1965. Not only had the new muscle Mustang been born, a whole new merchandising strategy began to take shape. Buyers could purchase a GT-350 right off the showroom floor, use it for day-to-day transportation, then go racing on the weekends!

With the 1965 Mustang production year wrapping up in late July and early August, a last-minute wave of 252 1965 model fastbacks made their way from San Jose to Shelby's plant in Los Angeles. Because the new and slightly revised 1966 model Mustangs would soon be hitting the streets, Shelby wasn't exactly thrilled with the idea of trying to sell last year's model, even if it was a fabled Shelby Mustang. The solution? Turn the 1965 cars into 1966 models. Essentially, the 252 last-minute Mustangs were fitted with new 1966 grilles and rear quarter window "Shelby-only" plexiglass. Although the cars still bore 1965 model VINs and warranty plates, they were refreshed with the new model year look. These 252 GT-350s are now referred to as changeover Shelby Mustangs.

For the 1966 model year production, GT-350s were slightly de-fanged. Oh, the Shelby-massaged 289 hi-po was still as potent as ever, but the car needed to be "humanized" a little bit. Ford and Shelby had both gotten feedback from customers and potential customers regarding the hard-edge 1965s. "It's only got two seats," "It's only available in white," "The exhaust and the differential are too loud," "The ride is too harsh," "How come only a four-speed?" were just some of the complaints.

For 1966, the GT-350s received a host of refinements and a relatively wide spectrum of five color choices. Hertz rental car company even stepped up and ordered 936 specially prepped and painted cars for their top-rated executive and business travelers to enjoy. These cars were officially identified by side panel striping that read "GT-350H."

All in all, including the cars built for Hertz, a total of 2,306 regular production GT-350 fast-

Above: 1965 Shelbys started out as 1965 fastbacks, hence the venting on the sail panel. Left: Special GT-350 side striping was somewhat reminiscent of the Mustang GT, but with Shelby's own flair.

Taillight panel "GT-350" emblem was subtle and to the point.

The 1966 Shelbys finally got their own unique gas caps. The 1965 cars simply used the stock Mustang gas cap. *Photo by*

backs were produced for 1966. Legend has it that six GT-350 convertibles slipped out of Shelby's plant just as the 1966 model year was wrapping up.

For 1966, Carroll Shelby withdrew his team from SCCA competition, since the big promotional racing effort had already paid off. Ford was happy: their performance goals had been achieved with the huge success of the first-generation Shelby GT-350s.

The official Shelby fender tag was pop-riveted over the existing VIN stamping. The tag design was the same for 1965 and 1966. *Photo by Tom Shaw*

Body and Exterior Trim

At first glance the 1965 Shelby GT-350 looked similar to a fastback GT. The Shelby Mustangs, however, were fitted with a lightweight fiberglass hood that sported a functional low-profile scoop. The standard Mustang grille had been cleaned up by removing the running horse and corral ornamentation, and by moving the classic Mustang tricolor bars and horse emblem to the left side of the grille. All other Mustang emblems were removed except for the stock gas cap located at the rear of the car. GT-350s were decorated with bold blue stripes that ran along the side of the car just above the rocker panels. And most of the 1965 Shelbys featured a small rectangular GT-350 emblem on the back of the rear taillight panel. The finishing touch was a pair of wide blue LeMans stripes that ran over the entire car, from front to rear valance panel.

Because the fiberglass hoods on 1965 Shelbys were prone to cracking (as any fiberglass hood would be), the hood springs on these cars were removed. They would have simply put too much pressure on the hood, possibly resulting in warping or splintering. This potential problem wouldn't be an issue for the 1966 Shelbys because they used a steel reinforced fiberglass hood.

COLOR PAINT CODES

	DuPont #	Ditzler#
For 1965 and 1965 changeover cars only:		
M = Wimbledon White	4480	8378
For 1966:		
M = Wimbledon White	4480	8378
A = Raven Black	88	9300
G = Sapphire Blue	4734	13075
T = Candyapple Red Apple Red	4737	71528
R = Ivy Green Metallic	4611	43408

Other than the obvious Mustang style revisions for 1966, the next-generation GT-350s also received brake-cooling quarter panel side vents and plexiglass rear quarter windows (in place of last year's standard sail panel louvers). On the six convertibles that were built in 1966, the rear quarter panel side vents were nonfunctional due to the convertible top mechanism. Because back-up lights were standard on 1966 Mustangs, they also became standard on the GT-350. The rear gas cap was now a special GT-350 cap, replacing the standard issue Mustang unit used on the 1965 Shelbys.

The phrase "You can have your Shelby in any color you like so long as it's Wimbledon White" was no longer true. GT-350s were available in Raven Black, Sapphire Blue, Candyapple Red, or Ivy Green Metallic. Oh, and yes, you could still order one in Wimbledon White.

Most of the special Hertz Shelbys were painted Raven Black with gold LeMans stripes, but approximately 200 or so were shipped to Hertz in a variety of the new hues.

The 1966 Shelby's side stripes were slightly narrower that the 1965s, and they were positioned a little higher on the car. Wimbledon White cars still got the blue stripes, while other colored Shelbys received white stripes.

Special Shelby American VIN Plate

Shelby GT-350s had a special "Shelby American" VIN plate that was applied to the inner fender well on both 1965 and 1966 cars. The vehicle warranty plate (located on the driver's door edge on all Mustangs) was removed by the Shelby plant, further stripping the Mustang of its identity. Although this modification solidified the fact that these were pure "Shelbys," it caused havoc in later years as the cars were brought in for servicing. All of Ford's original identifying marks had been erased.

General Specifications
Assembly Plant
All 1965 and 1966 Shelby GT-350s started out life at the Ford manufacturing plant in San Jose, California. They became "Shelby-ized" at Shelby American, Inc., Los Angeles, California.

Body
All 1965 and 1966 Shelby GT-350s were the fastback Mustang body style. Approximately six convertibles were made late in the 1966 model year.

Engine
For 1965 and 1966 model years, the GT-350's engine was the 289-2V V-8, Shelby-modified.

The 1965 Shelby GT-350 interior started out life as a stock Mustang interior and was transformed into a street-legal racecar. Shelby's special monster tach and oil pressure gauges were contained in their own special pod affixed to the indent atop the dash pad.

As the steering wheel design changed for 1966 Shelbys, so did the center cap, albeit ever so slightly.
Photo by Tom Shaw

Above: For 1965, the weighty rear seat was removed and a lightweight fiberglass molding was put in its place. The spare tire was now positioned directly over the rear wheels for added traction.

Above right: Heavy-duty racing-style seat belts replaced the existing stock ones.

Right: The 1966 Shelby GT-350 interior. Once again based on the K-code–equipped Mustang, the Shelby received the high-ranking 140-mph speedo (below left).

Far right: The pod tach was gone for 1966 and replaced with a single large tach center-mounted on the dash pad.
Photos by Tom Shaw

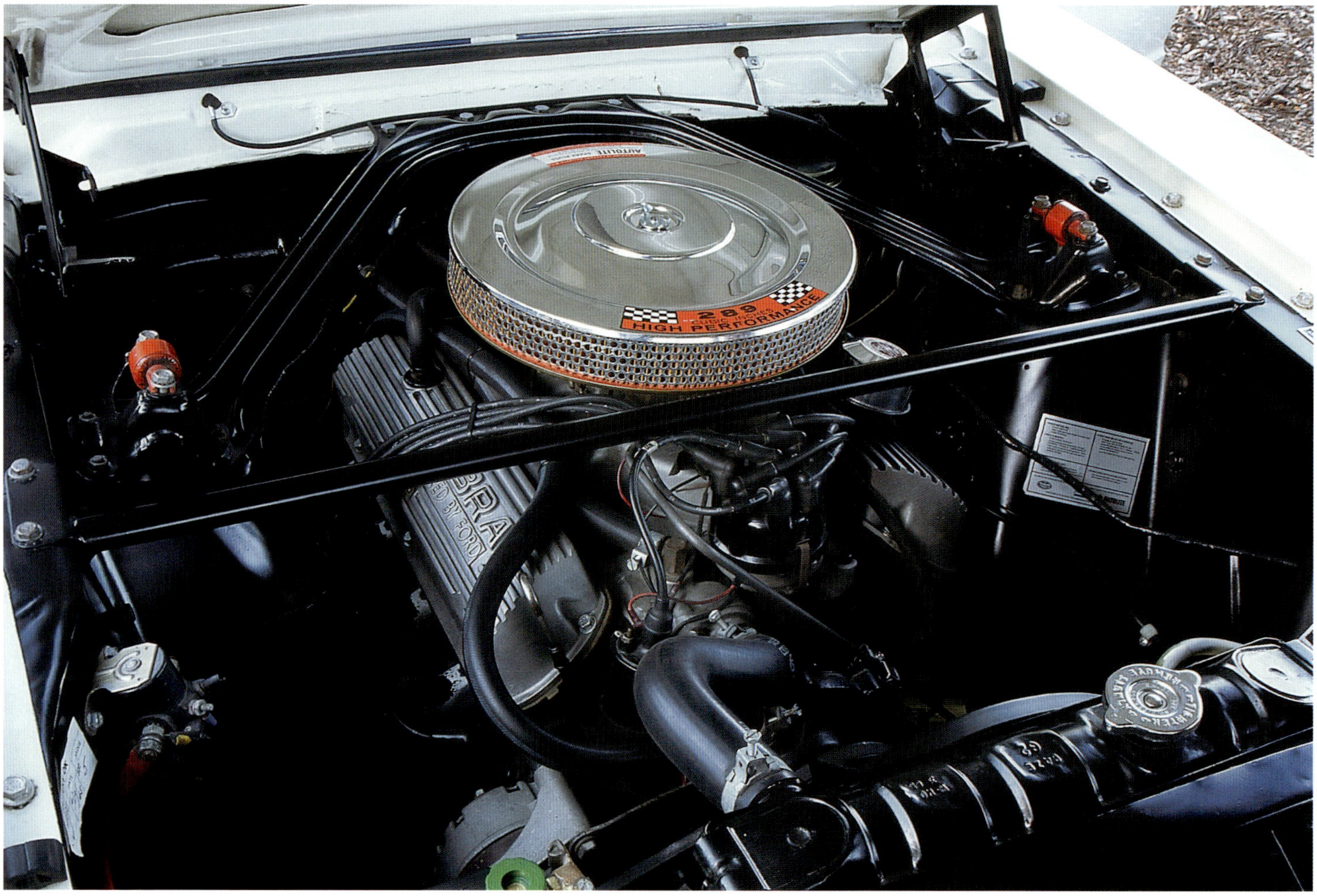

Consecutive Unit Number
All 1965 and 1966 GT-350s were identified by serial numbers assigned at Shelby American, Inc.

Interior
Standard Mustang interior was used for both 1965 and 1966 model years.

Trim
Trim for the standard interior was black.

Transmission
For 1965, the transmission came as a four-speed manual (Borg-Warner). For 1966, either a four-speed manual (Borg-Warner) or a C-4 dual-range Cruise-O-Matic (Ford) was used.

Interior

All 1965 models were based on the standard Mustang interior and were available in black only. The specially designed steering wheel was a flat, three-spoke aluminum piece with a wood rim. The unique Shelby designed "pod" affixed to the top of the dash pad was used to house a large 8,000-rpm tach and oil pressure gauge. Three-inch wide racing style seat belts were standard.

Top: The 1965 K-code 289-4V was specially modified and prepped by Carroll and his boys. Above: Fiberglass Shelby hoods didn't latch like conventional hoods. They were locked in place with hood pins.

The all-Ford Corporate Blue block should tell you it is a 1966 K-code 289. It is from the Hertz car, which, like the 1965s, was treated to a dose of Shelby magic.

The 1965 models were "rear seat delete" and instead featured a one-piece fiberglass rear shelf. The fire extinguisher shown in the photo on page 122 was added by the car's owner. It was not an official Shelby item.

For the 1966 model year, the GT-350s came equipped with the new-for-1966 Mustang interior, which featured the standard Ford five-gauge layout. Because the new instrument panel featured an oil pressure gauge, Shelby no longer needed to provide one. The center-mounted dash pod that was featured on the 1965s was axed, and a large 9,000-rpm tach was affixed to the top of the dash pad in its place. The 1966 steering wheel was the stock Mustang's optional deluxe walnut unit, with simulated wood trim. The center hub was replaced with a special Shelby cap that featured the same GT-350 logo that appeared on the rear gas cap.

Due to consumer demand, the fastback's folding rear seat made a comeback on the 1966 GT-350s and became a standard feature. A small number (probably fewer than 100) of the early 1966 cars came with the rear fiberglass unit used on the 1965 cars.

Chassis

Although several suspension modifications were made to both 1965 and 1966 Shelbys, the basic Mustang platform chassis was carried over intact.

Engine

For both the 1965 and 1966 model years, GT-350s were equipped with only one engine: the high-revving K-code 289 Hi-Performance four-barrel. Because we are concerned here with original features, we won't get into covering the Shelby race-prepped engines. Suffice it to say that they underwent several modifications that enabled them to pump out well over 350 horsepower.

When prepping the street versions, Shelby American took the stock 289 Ford hi-po motor and retrofit it with several unique parts that would let it easily hold its own against the fast-growing street muscle population. A specially designed all-aluminum high-rise intake manifold was combined with a 715-cubic-feet-per-minute Holley four-barrel carburetor, and finned aluminum Cobra valve covers replace the stock hi-po units. An extra-capacity aluminum oil pan and special high-flow Tri-Y exhaust headers rounded out the under-the-hood modifications.

For 1966, the only engine changes were those determined by Ford, and they were simply cosmetic in nature. Ford Corporate Blue paint was applied to all engines, including the ones shipped to Carroll Shelby.

All 1965 and 1966 GT-350s also received a Monte Carlo bar (named after the piece used on Falcons for the European Rally) that was used to tie the two front shock towers together. And instead of Ford's standard two-piece shock-tower brace that tied the towers back to the firewall, a single-piece support brace was used to provide an extra measure of rigidity to the car's front end.

Exhaust

The special Tri-Y header exhaust manifolds were connected to an H-pipe located near the base of the transmission housing. Then, dual exhaust pipes ran back along the length of the chassis where they fit into two separate glass-packed "bullet" mufflers that were located in front of the rear axle. On the 1965 models, the pipes exited the mufflers and dumped out just in front of the rear wheels. On 1966 Shelbys, the exhaust pipes ran the full length of the car and exited beneath the rear valance panel.

Transmissions

For 1965, the only transmission available was a four-speed Borg-Warner T-10 aluminum case unit

STANDARD EQUIPMENT ENGINE: K-CODE	
Type:	Eight-cylinder, 90-degree V, overhead valve
Displacement:	289 cubic inches
Foundry group:	Fairlane V8
Gross horsepower at 6,000 rpm:	306
Gross torque at 4,200 rpm:	329 ft.-lbs.
Valve lifters:	Solid/adjustable
Carburetor:	Holley, 4V (715 cfm.)
Recommended fuel:	Super Premium

with close gear ratios. Due to popular demand, 1966 Shelbys could be ordered with a Ford C-4 automatic transmission. The manually shifted Borg-Warner four-speed was still standard equipment.

The downside to ordering an automatic transmission–equipped GT-350 was that you said goodbye to the Holley carburetor. All automatic cars received an Autolite 595-cubic-feet-per-minute unit.

Rear Axles

For 1965, the rear axles were large 9-inch units equipped with a Detroit Automotive "No-Spin" ratcheting differential. For 1966, the 9-inch rear

From the Springtime Yellow convertible, this 1966 K-code motor sports an air conditioning unit. In a Shelby, yet! Near the end of 1966 production, a handful of Shelby convertibles were built. Obviously this one slipped out with a few amenities. *Photo by Tom Shaw*

end was still standard, but it was an open-type unit. The "Detroit Locker" also became an option.

Driveshaft and Universal Joints

All cars featured an exposed driveshaft with universal joints at either end. The driveshafts were made with seamless steel tubing to provide maximum strength and little added weight. Forged yokes were welded on at both ends, then the unit was precision balanced.

Universal joints were the cross-and-yoke type, featuring sealed, prelubricated needle bearings. Service was required at 36,000-mile intervals.

Suspension

The 1965 model GT-350s featured suspensions that were modified with full 1-inch front stabilizer bars, special pitman and idler arms, lowered upper control (A) arms, Koni brand adjustable shocks, and rear override traction bars. Special suspension travel-limiting cables were affixed to the rear axle housing.

For 1966, after much public outcry over the harsh ride, Shelby elected to dispense with several of the earlier suspension modifications. The upper control arms were left at their stock Mustang height, the Koni shocks became an option (now standard were heavy-duty Ford shock absorbers), and the rear traction bars were replaced with simpler underride units.

The 1965 model Shelbys used trunk-mounted batteries for better weight distribution. Although this placement worked nicely, several customers began complaining about battery acid leaks eating through their trunk mats. For 1966, the batteries were relocated to the engine compartment.

Brakes

For 1965 and 1966 model GT-350s, the front brakes were large four-piston caliper Ford disc units. Galaxie station wagon drum brakes were used out back. Both front and rear brakes used sintered metallic linings.

Cooling

All GT-350s received heavy-duty, 14-quart radiators that were fully pressurized and thermostatically controlled. Thermostats were located at the upper engine outlet. Fans were four-bladed, and radiator shrouds were used to enhance the cooling effect.

Wheels and Tires

For 1965, the standard GT-350 wheel was a 15"x5½" station wagon rim that was painted silver and included chrome lug nuts. Early 1966 Shelbys used the 1965 Cragar-style mag wheels until the supply ran out. Then the standard wheel was a 14-inch Magnum 500-style wheel that was painted gray with black centers.

Below left: Optional wheels for 1966 Shelbys were either the new aluminum 10-spoke or a chromed version of Magnum 500–style wheel (see the Hertz GT-350H featured). Both were 14 inches.

Below right: The optional Shelby wheel for 1965 was a 15-inch Cragar-style mag wheel. Although rarely sighted, a 15-inch steel wheel was standard.

Index